Mending Softly

Finding Hope and Healing After Ectopic Pregnancy Loss

By

Jodi Sky Rogers

2020

Titles also by Jodi Sky Rogers

Fertility Calm Creative Journal

Daily Cup of Fertility Calm: Tea Meditations, Inspiration and Self-Care Practices For Anxiety Relief During The Two Week Wait

Flowering Within: A Journey to Feminine Healing & Grace

Wild Essence: Return to the Peace & Freedom of Your Inner Wilderness

Essays Featured in the Following Anthologies

A Tea Reader: Living Life One Cup At A Time (by Katrina Avila Munchiello)

Wild and Precious: A Guide to Loving Yourself, Following Your Bliss, and Changing the World (Curated by Wild Sister Magazine)

Spiritual Awakenings: The Many Paths to Connection (by Angela Raspass)

This is Pregnancy and Baby Loss (by Sheila Lamb)

Mending Softly

Copyright © 2020 Jodi Sky Rogers

All rights reserved. No part of this book may be utilized or reproduced in any form or by any means, electronic or mechanical, including photocopying, recording, taping or by other information storage and retrieval system without the written permission of the author, except in the case of brief quotations embodied in critical or reference articles and reviews.

Visit My Website: https://jodiskyrogers.com

Instagram: @thefertilemoon

ISBN: 9798690663957

Dedication

To our Angel Baby

To the warrior women who have walked this path

To my darling husband, thank you for your undying love and support

To incredible family and friends who held space for us and supported us throughout our healing journey

Contents

Preface 9

Endings and Beginnings 14

The Calm Before the Storm 20

The Devastating News 30

Surrendering to the Inevitable 35

The Aftermath 41

The Hands of the Mender 49

A Silent Prayer 53

40 Days of Healing 56

Allowing Rest 64

Grief Release Ceremony 68

Learning to Focus on the Things that are Thriving 73

The Second Wave: Dealing with PTSD and Anxiety ... 84

Healing the Trauma 92

Healing as a Couple 106

The Due Date 119

Post Traumatic Growth 130

Making Room for Hope 140

Hashtags For Your Journey

#mendingsoftly

#jodiskyrogers

#ectopicpregnancysurvivor

#ectopicpregnancyawareness

#soulfulfertility

#healingafterectopicloss

#healingafterpregnancyloss

Sherd

[Noun] 1) *a variant of shard, 2) a pottery shard, 3) a broken piece of a brittle artefact*

Preface

"Imagine that your life before infertility was a vase. One day a loss or trauma tips that beautiful vase to the ground. Tiny and large shards of glass are everywhere. What are you going to do with these glass shards?"

~ Joanna Flemons

I wish I'd fallen softly. Light and graceful like a feather drifting slowly to the earth on a warm and dreamy summer's day. I wish that I'd landed softly too. But there is nothing soft or graceful about that devastating moment when the worst has come to pass. The unavoidable truth is that it is hard, cold and brutal. All that you know to be true and good in life shatters in an instant. You feel like a delicate pottery bowl violently tossed from your place of rest, watching yourself crash and scatter across the hostile dark earth. The sound is deafening. Time stops. Inside, the quiet ache of shock and heartbreak slowly makes its grip known. They cut deep, these jagged edges of broken sherds. You gasp for air hungrily, yet somehow forget how to breathe.

'Is there any point in breathing if this is what the world is asking me to face?' You think to yourself.

Somehow though, whether through madness or magic, you find a way to. You keep breathing even when you don't think you can. You surprise yourself.

The fall is hard – the crashing, the breaking, the scattering of your broken clay body. What I found however, is that the mending is slow, soft and although somewhat ungraceful still, you sense yourself being held by an unseen force, something greater than you wrapping you in its balm. Remember this on those days when it feels like healing will never come. Perhaps it is true that you may never be the same again going forward. Innocence is lost after all, the innocence of blind hope and the innocence of a joyful or easy pregnancy. While I don't want to diminish the depth of your hurt, trauma and fear of an uncertain future, I do want to offer a glimmer of hope for the possibility of finding healing and wholeness beyond the pain. No one likes hearing that healing comes with time, but the truth is that it does.

Over the years, I've read many stories about how ancient sherds of broken pottery are mended. In the aftermath of my ectopic pregnancy loss I kept revisiting literature about this mending process with great fascination for reasons I couldn't understand. There's a slow and mindful art to carefully piecing back together each sherd in order to recreate the remnants of what the original artefact once was. A deeply thoughtful and somewhat intuitive art, if you will.

Something in this process of mending broken pottery seemed to resonate in the context of my quest for hope and healing. I couldn't pinpoint exactly why at first, but the deeper I reached in search of meaning, the more clearly I saw just how it mirrored my own unravelling and how it offered itself as a metaphor for my potential to mend myself. Each individual piece with its distinct shape, with its unique lines and curves is a memoir of its own, a tale of what was before. Like a quiet whisper it narrates the story of the devastating blow that was dealt and gives insight into how things fell apart. Then comes the restoration, the time laboured effort to gently rebuild what's been broken. The act of mending asks three important things of you – patience, trust and surrender. The fractures, the cracks, the staples and the revealing swaths of glue stand out boldly like the wounds in my heart and soul that cannot be hidden from sight. And the missing pieces, those gaping holes are anecdotes of the things that are lost forever – my baby, my fallopian tube, a piece of my dignity and fertility – the things you learn to live without. Or perhaps I should say the things that you learn to carry on living for in spite of what has happened, because through surrender and acceptance you discover the power of your personal strength and resilience. Something profound happens when you wake up in a calm green pasture on the other side of the treacherous storm that you thought would end you. You discover who you are beyond the unimaginable. You discover what you are made of. Suddenly, the thing that may have broken you becomes the very thing that empowers and emboldens you.

Granted, this is difficult to imagine when you are at your lowest point. However, in the moment of my deepest despair I found myself faced with a choice – either I would sink even lower into the dark and scary place I felt I was losing myself to, or I could find a way to reach towards life. The depths of depression scared me more than the idea of living. Ultimately, I wanted my would-have-been-baby to mean something and for their memory not to be swallowed by a black hole of persistent misery. So, I began my path to mending softly, willing myself to breathe again, moment to moment. I've had to dig deep to re-establish my sense of self and unearth the person I had become on the other side of tragedy. Writing this book has been part of my heart's mending. I offer the words upon these pages in the hope that sharing my story with you as honestly as I can will bring some kind of comfort to you on your own quest for healing. I want you to know that you are not alone, darling heart. I walk this road with you. While I don't know how the rest of the journey will unfold or how either of ours will end, I do know that we are both survivors and thrivers. Keep breathing. May you find your place of peace through you own process of mending softly.

PART ONE

The Meandering Journey

Endings and Beginnings

"Every closed chapter is the starting point for a new story. Whatever is ending, let it end. That is how all beautiful things begin." ~ Martha Beck

It's hard to know where to begin. In reality, I've had so many beginnings and so many moments where I'd thought I'd finally come to my story's happy conclusion only to find myself starting over again. One could say that there were already cracks forming in the pitcher, even before it was tossed to the earth. The scars of life, pregnancy loss and subfertility were like fault lines digging ridges into my flesh. I felt the ripples and the subtle crevices that they kept carving into me, and mended them where I could. Even so, there is no denying that they were there.

Thinking back, I don't remember too much about what I expected in the beginning of our fertility journey. I vaguely recall feeling excited about reaching a place of readiness, excited at the prospect of becoming a mother. That readiness rose in me as a surprising yet profound internal shift, an eagerness to step forward from my blissfully familiar experience of maidenhood into the wild unknown of motherhood. I was naturally maternal at a young age. I felt a responsibility to nurture those around me. I was a 'mother hen' to friends, always concerned about their wellbeing and doing what I could to be helpful. I loved babysitting and looking after my cousins during the holidays. So I knew, like most women do, that having and caring for my own children was an obvious part of the plan for my adult life. There was no question about it.

There was a lot of change happening in our lives when my husband and I decided that we were ready to grow our family. I'd left behind a career in the environmental and social development field to become a spiritual life coach. My husband and I had been married for almost five years at that point and he'd finally made the move away from business and property journalism to pursue his passion as a sports journalist and a professional keynote speaker. We were preparing to move out of our one bedroom city apartment to a lovely two-bedroom place with a garden. So, the timing just seemed right.

Like so many, I must have expected this journey to be a whole lot easier than what it has turned out to be. After all, from the moment we met, from our very first conversation, most things about 'us' and our relationship have always flowed with ease. My husband and I met on the first day of orientation week as new students at University. We simply connected in a very special way. I'll add that I've always been pragmatic and cynical, so the idea of forming a meaningful relationship and falling in love that early in my life was the furthest thing from my mind. Yet, it happened. We just fitted so perfectly into each other's lives and simple things like his gentle, wise and loving nature, our shared values and the way we complemented one another made it a joy to cultivate a loving soul connection that has now blossomed into almost 12 years of marriage. So, why wouldn't trying to start a family happen with the same level of ease? If only I'd known.

It was a challenge from the get go. The first month of our trying to conceive (TTC) began with a chemical pregnancy and then being diagnosed with polycystic ovarian syndrome (PCOS), insulin resistance and unusually high testosterone levels shortly afterwards - ominous signs of what was to come. I spent the next year doing follow-up check-ups, going up and down to the endocrinologist I was referred to, doing various tests, bloodwork, an MRI and not getting any answers or clear direction. My endocrinologist was
convinced that my hormones where out of whack because I had a tumor. After enduring several scary tests, no tumor was found. I was then told that I most probably had a congenital adrenal dysfunction of some sort. Again, after a few months of going through various tests, nothing was found. I consulted a nutritionist and focused on doing what

I could to enhance my fertility. It was a very frustrating and confusing time where I felt as though my life was on hold. I endeavoured to keep doing everything that I was told to do, yet it didn't seem to be making much of a difference. It was disheartening because, despite all the work I was putting in, I lost very little weight and could not fall pregnant. I also felt very isolated, since I didn't know of anyone else who was going through what I was. What I know now, is that unfortunately the practitioners tending to me had little insight into PCOS and did not have the best understanding of how to help me bring my body back into balance (*fortunately things have since changed and there is a lot more information and support available to women with PCOS now*). As a consequence, I had very little information to work with on my own. Nevertheless, I did the best that I could with the information that I had and tried to stick with what I thought was the healthiest lifestyle for me.

After a tumultuous first year and a long relaxing December holiday, I finally fell pregnant in the January of the New Year. Shocked, excited and in awe of how things had fallen into place, we were so grateful for the blessing. Alas, after days of cramping and spotting, sadly I began miscarrying before my 8 week scan. That miscarriage marked the beginning of a downward spiral. The weight of subfertility had taken its toll on me. My self-esteem and self-worth were completely eroded. I was exhausted from constantly moving through cycles of hopefulness, excitement, disappointment, frustration and grief. I fell into depression. I abandoned my health efforts, threw myself into my work and avoided looking at my own pain. I gained back the weight that I'd lost and more. Deep down I still really wanted a baby, I wanted desperately to become a mother. But I felt wounded and so afraid that it wouldn't happen for me. I felt so naïve and guilty for having wasted time and not recognizing that I would most likely face fertility challenges sooner.

Fortunately for me, I eventually had a turning point about five years ago. I guess I'd hit rock bottom and reached a place where I knew that I could no longer allow things to carry on the way they had been. I felt so low, unhealthy and the possibility of having our baby felt so far way. Since I was a life coach, I recognized that I already had the tools and resources to make a positive life change in my hands. I decided to take the opportunity to apply what I had been learning and practicing with my clients to what I was struggling with in the context of my own fertility journey. I couldn't leave my fertility in the hands of other people anymore. So, I began empowering and educating myself more. I made drastic lifestyle changes, found supportive TTC communities, changed doctors, found an amazing fertility Naturopath/Acupuncturist and enlisted the help of a Wellness coach who had a lot better insight into PCOS than my previous nutritionist. Things seemed to align better and it was as if the Universe brought the right people and practitioners into my life. Having the right kind of support has made all the difference. My Naturopath was so thorough. She took steps to test and monitor all my reproductive hormones and then advise wellness and lifestyle changes accordingly, something that none of my previous doctors had done. I felt empowered, supported and as though I was finally on the right track. The prospect of being pregnant and expecting the arrival of my beautiful blessing didn't seem so impossible anymore. I felt as though my string of disappointments would eventually be over and I would enter an era of new beginnings.

The Calm Before the Storm

"Sometimes pain was like a storm that came out of nowhere. The clearest summer could end in a downpour. Could end in lightning and thunder."

~ Benjamin Alire Sáenz

It's happened before, those quiet whisperings that came just before I discovered that I'd been gifted something special. With the pregnancy that I miscarried in 2014, I had dreams about my baby. I dreamt that I was pregnant weeks before it actually happened. The dream brought with it an air of certainty that I couldn't shake. I knew intuitively that something was coming. This time around wasn't any different. The incoming life seemed to announce itself a few weeks before my pregnancy was a reality. In my confusion, I wasn't sure what to make of it. I'd been let down so many times previously that I was afraid to trust it. But the whispers made themselves known in subtle ways.

"Your beautiful blessing is on its way," they said.

I'll never forget the calm and precious moments of bliss before it all shattered, they were truly magical even in the midst of uncertainty and fear. I began 2019 in a really good space. We had a lovely festive season with our family and friends. I felt healthy, vibrant and was so close to reaching my goal weight. I had discovered aerial yoga a couple of months earlier and had completely fallen in love with it. I'd also started doing belly dance classes, something that I'd always wanted to do. For the first time in a long time I felt so happy, like I was thriving and as though things were flowing beautifully in many areas of my life.

I was feeling somewhat despondent about my TTC journey at the same time, though not entirely discouraged. Although I was ready to hit the ground running at the start of a new and exciting year, we were forced to take a break for a couple of months as we worked to rebuild our savings – all the supplements, appointments, wellness workshops, my regular acupuncture and naturopathic sessions, frequent hormone monitoring blood tests and other fertility care efforts had become quite expensive to maintain. The media company that my husband worked for at the time was also undergoing restructuring, putting him at risk of being retrenched. So it made sense for us to plan for that unfortunate possibility and create a secure buffer for ourselves. That meant being more frugal and sacrificing many of the things that we'd usually spend on.

The situation was far from ideal, but we put one foot in front of the other and made the best of what we had. Naturally, there were low moments when I felt so frustrated, however, for the most part I did my best to focus my energy on my health, my wellbeing and the things that brought me joy as often as I could. It was easy to find fulfilment in the things that I enjoyed doing – spending time with friends and their kids, getting out in nature, the aerial yoga and dance classes and having fun with some creative work projects.

As if on cue, a fertility coach, whose work I admire and have followed for several years, announced that she would be running a free online fertility mindset programme. The timing of it was perfect. While I had to stop many of the things I usually did to support my body and fertility, her offering presented a chance to be more still and relax into the mental, emotional and spiritual side of things. It was a reminder to take a break from 'doing' and attune to the more passive energy of 'being'. She ran the online programme over the course of six weeks, and it was a really wonderful experience. I listened to so many insightful talks from leading fertility experts and functional medicine practitioners who offered loads of useful advice and resources. They reinforced important lessons that I was starting to lose sight of in my despondency, reminding me to focus my attention on my inner wellbeing during my period of limbo. Participating in this programme allowed me to do some needed inner work, and to shift my mindset around my fertility and my ideas of motherhood. I resumed with the soul nurturing practices that I'd been neglecting in those recent months. I journaled, did early morning yoga and worked with my fertility affirmations daily. I got back into my evening routine of doing self-fertility massage and a meditation before bed. As a consequence, my sleep patterns improved and I woke up feeling more refreshed and well rested. The stress of not being able to control every aspect of my fertility journey lessened. I felt calm and there was this underlying sense that something wonderful was unfolding.

A couple of weeks later when I woke up on my 37th birthday, it was a dark, gloomy overcast day. I was somewhat surprised not to feel as excited as I thought I would. Despite how well I'd been doing, something about it felt bittersweet. Although I had many good things to celebrate, I was also acutely aware of my advancing age. I was edging closer to forty and there was a baby-shaped hole in my life still waiting to be filled. It wasn't so much about getting older as it was about the fear of my fertility window closing and my childbearing years escaping me. Those who struggle with subfertility would understand that a piece of your heart breaks a little when you turn another year older without your hoped-for-baby in your arms. You can't help feeling that you've missed a whole year of opportunities to get pregnant and have a baby.

I've a vague recollection of that day. My husband, ever gentle, thoughtful and attuned to my state of emotion, had planned a day filled with birthday surprises. We had a cake by candlelight for breakfast early that morning. Then around mid-morning my husband whisked me off to a secret venue. It turned out to be one of my favourite places, a popular art gallery. There was something about the ambience of the gallery that's always felt like stepping into a dreamland of sorts. Its spaciousness, the white walls and their incredible selection of curated pieces resonated with me. I walked around the gallery gleefully taking in the beauty of my surrounds. We examined and appreciated the new paintings and sculptures, discussing our impressions of the various pieces. Suddenly, I found myself standing in front of a portrait that just took my breath way. I stopped dead in my tracks and a palpable silence enveloped me. It was a portrait of a young boy. The vibrant colours drew me in. It turned out to be a painting by Nelson Makamo, an incredible South African artist who had had one of his portraits published on the cover of Time magazine a few months early. There was something about the emotion in the boy's eyes that moved me. A space inside of me opened up and I felt a deep connection to something beyond the painting, a connection to an essence, to what felt like my future child. I felt their presence so strongly and had this intense and inexplicable knowing that they were near me.

"My babies are coming soon," said a quiet voice inside me.

Taken aback, my eyes welled up. Looking at the painting, I wondered if I'd caught a glimpse of what my one day baby would look like.

"Perhaps it was a sign that I would be pregnant soon," I thought.

I really wanted that to be true.

Over the course of the next few weeks, one menstrual cycle ended and a new one began. I continued the gentle self-care and mindfulness practices to support my general wellbeing and my fertility. Something about my experience at the gallery calmed me. Feeling a very real spiritual connection to my baby reassured me. It made me trust that there was a baby out there waiting to become mine and that it was just a matter of time. The unshakable sureness was reinforced one Saturday afternoon, when the movement studio where I'd been taking classes hosted a sound healing meditation workshop. It was the first time I'd ever attended something like that and it was a lovely experience. The vibrations and sounds of the crystal bowls and koshi chimes were so soothing. During the workshop, the facilitator guided us through a relaxing visualization. At some point during the meditation, in my mind's eye, I saw myself and my husband surrounded by a dark star-studded sky, and then a beautiful soft pink swirl of energy came down from the stars and into our arms to join us. My heart filled will love. I felt strongly that this was a clear message from our baby.

The week after the sound healing workshop I was completely exhausted. Distracted by a friend's bridal shower, her wedding, some birthday celebrations and trying to get work done in between, I couldn't quite figure out why I was struggling to find the energy to get things done. I'd overslept almost every morning even though I'd gone to bed earlier than usual. I had strange and vivid dreams every night. My 'PMS' symptoms were way more pronounced than they usually are. My boobs were hurting and had swelled so much that my sports bras didn't fit. When my period was late, I took a pregnancy test. It was negative, a false negative, something that I later learned is common with ectopic pregnancies. I was confused as to what was going on with my body, especially since I'd been managing my diet, lifestyle and PCOS symptoms really well. *"Why would I suddenly have an irregular cycle?"* I wondered

When another week had passed with still no sign of my period, I decided to take another home pregnancy test expecting that it would probably be negative again. This time, the pregnancy test was positive. I was shocked. I took another test later that day to be sure it was actually positive. Three more home pregnancy tests later and they all turned out to be positive. My husband and I were so excited. It's strange sometimes how our beliefs affect us. Even though intuitively I'd sensed that something was coming, I didn't expect that it would happen so soon. I had a hard time believing that it was real. The next day, we made an appointment with our GP to get bloodwork done. We were so nervous. The bloodwork results came back the same day and confirmed that I was indeed just over 5 weeks pregnant. We were overjoyed. The connection that I felt was real after all. The signs that I was too afraid to acknowledge were not a figment of my imagination. Next, I tried to get an appointment with an Obygyn. No one would see me sooner than 10 weeks into the pregnancy. I called around to several different doctors and eventually I booked the earliest date that I could find at around 8/9 weeks.

In the meantime, the calm that rose from my center deepened. It flowed outward like a serene tranquility that I've never known. Unlike past pregnancies that I miscarried, I had no pain, no cramping and no bleeding. Everything felt right. I let the calm essence guide me through my days as I ate to nourish myself and my baby and enjoyed gentle yoga to keep me grounded each morning. I took the pregnancy journal that I had bought for myself the previous December out from the cupboard. I was excited that I was finally getting to use it to document my daily emotions and experiences. When returned to my Naturopath for acupuncture sessions, I felt so good about the fact that I was nurturing my body and baby through morning sickness, fatigue and a whole host of early pregnancy symptoms.

There's one particular evening during that time that still lays freshly in my mind. It was the night of a full moon, and the autumn equinox also happened to fall on the same day. Our garden was luminous in moon glow, so my husband and I decided to go outside and enjoy the moon touched air that evening. We stood on the soft grass looking up at the night sky as the cool newly autumn breeze settled on our skin. The garden was a dreamy mix of floral scents – the passionfruit daisies, salvia and my pink 'David Austin' roses all rolled into one to create a unique signature perfume of its own. At one point, my husband wrapped his arms around me and held me for a long while. My heart overflowed with love and gratitude. Our energies had melded together to create a new life. As we stood there, wrapped in embrace, it wasn't just the two of us, we were three. We were a family.

Not too long ago, my husband and I took a trip to London. While there, we visited an art gallery with a Korean ceramics exhibition on display. The exhibition included a stunning collection of 'moon jars' by Korean ceramist, Ree Soo Jong. Traditionally, to make a 'moon jar' (which is said to be named for its shape and colour), the ceramist throws two individual bowls and then carefully joins these delicate individual pieces together to form one big imperfectly spherical jar. The area where the two pots are joined is smoothed out and the jar is then painted and glazed to create a beautiful big spheroid vessel. Ree Soo Jong's moon jars were painted lovely neutral shades of white and earthy browns. There was something about them that reminded me of us in that precious moment standing under the moonlit sky. Two souls merged, delicate hearts carefully smoothed and joined in the hope of creating one big life together. We were whole and our moon jar was full with both the love and the tiny life we were bringing into the world. I revisit that moment often just to stand in the beauty of the calm before the storm that was about to sweep through our lives. Nothing could have prepared me for what came next.

The Devastating News

"During this part of the journey, the woman begins her descent. It may involve a seemingly endless period of wandering, grief, and rage; of dethroning kings; of looking for the lost pieces of herself and meeting the dark feminine." ~ Maureen Murdock

It was an incredibly tense moment. My husband stood in the room with me as the doctor conducted our first pre-natal scan. We were anxious and excited all at once. Unlike our last pregnancy loss, this time things felt different. There was no indication of a problem. My early pregnancy symptoms were in full effect. So, I had every reason to be hopeful.

The doctor seemed rather quiet. All three of us had our eyes fixed on the monitor as she searched for signs of life. It seemed to be taking a while. Eventually, she moved the scanner to my right side, and then we saw it, a little sac with a foetal pole – *my baby*. The doctor zoomed in on the monitor to see our baby more clearly. A little flash that flickered on the monitor screen quickly revealed itself to be my baby's heartbeat. It was quite honestly the most precious thing I've ever seen. She turned up the volume on the monitor and the room filled with the sound of our baby's strong and beautiful heart. Overcome with a deep sense of joy, I glanced over at my husband excitedly. I saw just how the sight and sound off the little thriving heart moved him. It was so surreal. Everything that we'd endured to that point seemed worth the profound joy that we'd shared in that moment.

We watched the monitor screen as the doctor moved the ultrasound scanner around again.

"My concern is that it doesn't look like there is anything in the uterus," she said.

I was confused. We'd just seen the baby. What did she mean?

She moved back to where the baby was. *"Here, I can see the sac with the foetal pole. And that is the heartbeat. But it looks like it's implanted in your right fallopian tube instead of the uterus."*

"I'm sorry my darling," she said, *"but I'm afraid this looks like an ectopic pregnancy."* She explained that this meant that the pregnancy was not viable, it was dangerous for me. She told me that my fallopian tube was mostly ruptured, which would cause internal bleeding, and the baby would not be able to grow or develop properly in the tube. The

best course of action was to have surgery to remove the fallopian tube.

'Ectopic pregnancy', I thought. I was stunned. I couldn't believe that this was happening after everything we'd been through. We'd worked so hard to get pregnant again. I looked at my husband. Something in me shattered further when I read the tell-tale signs of heartbreak across his face. There was no hiding how crushed he was. *'Had I made a mistake bringing him here?'* I wondered. It seemed cruel now that I had given him a moment to catch a glimpse of life on the monitor, the baby's heart still flickering wildly before our eyes. *'Why had I put him in this devastating place where for a moment he may have believed that together we'd finally created something so beautiful?'* I thought. It felt like such a selfish thing to have done. My heart sunk lower and lower. The internal resistance kicked in. I wrestled with myself. I wrestled with the situation. I didn't want to accept it. *'This couldn't be real,'* I told myself. We were supposed to be celebrating good news, not facing the reality of losing another pregnancy. My baby was meant to be due on my husband's birthday. I wanted to be pregnant and give birth to a healthy baby so badly.

I got dressed and then sat down next to my husband in the doctor's office. He asked her to explain what this meant. I felt detached from my body, watching the situation from somewhere out there. The doctor laid out the options. She suggested opting for surgery rather than the medical treatment route (the methotrexate shot) considering that my fallopian tube had ruptured and the advanced developmental stage of the baby. She needed us to make the decision as soon as possible so that she could schedule the surgery. I could see that my husband was in denial as he kept asking more questions and tried to get his head around the idea that nothing could be done to save the baby, and then the rush of fear when he understood that on top of everything else, this was potentially a dangerous situation for me. I guess denial would be an apt word to sum up where we both found ourselves. I understood what the doctor was saying, but it still felt like a mistake. I didn't have any of the symptoms that women are said to experience with ectopic pregnancies. I wasn't bleeding. I wasn't in pain. I felt pregnant. I still had nausea and all the pregnancy symptoms. *'She must have made a mistake,'* I thought. In contrast to past pregnancies where I miscarried early, it just didn't *feel* like anything was wrong.

Walking out of the doctor's office was one of the most humiliating experiences. I tried my best to put on a smile as we re-entered a waiting room full of both newly pregnant and heavily, almost full-term, pregnant women, making our way to the receptionist to ensure that our medical insurance had settled the appointment expenses. Their joy, anxiety, anticipation and the fullness of some of their bellies reflected everything that I longed for but was now being taken away. I didn't want them to see my brokenness and my pain. I didn't want them to see my failure.

This was the beginning of my shattering, a long and painful process of my heart, my life and my body being ripped apart. Every instinct in me wanted to resist it, to fight as hard as I could for another way out. But already more deep cracks had formed themselves in the clay body of my being and the sherds of my existence were crumbling to the floor. In her book, Broken Places & Outer Spaces, in which author Nnedi Okorafor writes about her experience of becoming paralyzed from the waist down after a back op went wrong, she calls it 'the breaking' – the inconceivable thing that breaks your life and your body. There was no way to stop it all from happening. Yet, it feels like you can't find your peace in surrendering to it either, and so for that period of time life feels like a kind of cruel and treacherous hell.

We went home devastated and I cried for hours. I felt so broken and scared that I would never be okay again.

Surrendering to the Inevitable

"Life is a balance between what we can control and what we cannot. I am learning to live between effort and surrender." ~ Danielle Orner

We lay on our bed, heart sore, the room dimly lit by our bedside lamps. Dark descended so quickly that evening. The grey skies and rain mirrored the sinking sense of melancholy that enveloped us. I had started my pregnancy in the dog days of summer. Now, it was so clear that summer was long gone, autumn had set in and ahead of us lay a long and hard winter.

We were unsure what to do with the news. So, we did the responsible thing. I called my mom to let her know. My husband called his mother first, and then his best friend. I sent a message to a handful of my close friends. I figured it was the considerate thing to do so that they would understand if I was not myself for a while. I didn't really want to talk to anyone. I turned my phone to silent and set it aside.

Moments later, something so unexpected happened. There was a buzz at our front gate. We hadn't been expecting anyone to visit. Just minutes after having sent to message, my friend, someone who had become a close soul sister in the short space of three years showed up at my house. I was taken aback. I hadn't asked for her to be there, but there she was. I went to the bathroom to clean myself up while my husband welcomed her in. I took a few moments to ground myself, still uncertain how to move through this unfamiliar territory. When I joined them in the living room, she greeted me with a hug, the long, warm and heartfelt kind that made me feel held and supported in a way that few people other than my husband have ever made me feel. She's always been a great hugger. My tension eased along with my unsureness, the uncertainty of how I was supposed to be or act in my moment of vulnerability. I felt her compassion. Tears flowed down my face in overwhelm.

She must have offered words of sympathy and encouragement, though I don't remember what she said. What I do remember is this – the love that I felt and how much it meant for someone to reach beyond the awkwardness and show up in such a meaningful way. The truth is that no one ever knows what to do or what to say to you when you're going through a trauma or experiencing a loss. It's always an uncomfortable situation, especially since, as the person going through the experience, you don't know how to *be* either. Our instinct is to withdraw, to create distance between ourselves and what we have to face. We put up a wall to shield ourselves and keep the people around us out because it feels easier. So, I was and remain deeply touched by her bravery and willingness to compassionately offer her support in the way that she did. I'd feared the embarrassment of breaking down and crying in front of my friend, my failure to sustain yet another pregnancy laid bare for all to see. Yet there, in the throes of emotion, I felt unexpectedly comforted. In her presence, something in me softened, my defenses lowered and I sensed myself surrender a little. I sat amidst my heart's broken sherds unable to hide the mess. I was unable to disguise my pain, control what was happening or how it looked from the outside. Accepting that I couldn't fight the inevitable felt a lot like defeat, but there was nothing I could do except just be where I was. It hurt terribly, but I didn't need to hide that. I didn't need to know how I was going to piece myself back together again at that moment. I just needed to allow myself to be supported.

I can't fully explain the medicine of sitting in shared company or why having someone hold my hand and bear witness to my pain made me feel like I'd find the strength to get to the other side of what I was going through, but it did. It didn't erase the hurt and anger or stop the tears from flowing, but it made me feel less alone. It was the comfort of knowing that someone was holding space for me at a time when my world was crashing.

Shortly before she left, I remember her saying: *'Love you always'*, a simple phrase that went straight to my heart. Those words had become our signoff when we messaged one another, words I'd offered to her on her bad days and during tough times to remind her that she had someone to lean on. They were words meant to reinforce that the depth of our friendship and the value of the sisterhood that we'd cultivated could be a source of strength to draw on when curveballs where flung her way. Hearing those words meant everything.

Later that night, I struggled to find sleep. I felt the black hole in my chest swallowing me, myself dissolving into the dark stormy night. I felt helpless. I couldn't protect our baby. I didn't understand why this was happening. My mind kept replaying the image of our baby on the hospital monitor, their beating heart and active little body doing everything that they could to grow and thrive. I was failing them. Somewhere between the sobs and sorrow that was eating away at me, I remembered a quote by Gabrielle Bernstein from her audiobook, 'The Universe Has Your Back', I'd been listening to. Bernstein said:

"When you think you've surrendered, surrender more."

As hard as it was, I knew that this was what the moment was calling for me to do. I couldn't will a different reality into being. I had to reach deeper and find it in me to *surrender more*. I shifted my focus to my breathing and the idea of surrendering to a devastating situation that I couldn't control. As I did, a thought struck me. I was still pregnant, and in the little time I had left I could still exercise my role as a mother by making sure that my baby felt comfortable and loved. So, I put on some calming meditation music with koshi chime sounds for a relaxing environment, placed my hands on my womb space and focused my intention on sending love to my baby. I expressed my gratitude for the few short weeks of joy that our baby brought into our lives. I let them know that they were so loved and wanted. I said a prayer asking for them to be surrounded by extra love and angels. It may sound strange to some, but I didn't want the only experience of life they would have to be wrapped up in stress and angst. I made a promise to myself that for the next day up until the surgery, I would do my best to remain calm and grounded in feelings of love. That was the only thing I felt I could offer my angel baby in that little time we had left, so that was what I did. I was very aware of the fact that not every woman who experiences an ectopic pregnancy knows upfront that she is pregnant. In many cases a big part of the trauma is being rushed to the emergency room in excruciating pain as a result of a ruptured tube only to find out there and then that they are pregnant, their life is at risk and they will have to lose the pregnancy. As devastating as my situation was, I also knew that I was blessed to have been gifted this time to connect with and appreciate the little soul that had chosen to be with me.

The next morning, I called my doctor to schedule the surgery. I requested one more scan to be absolutely sure that it was in fact an ectopic pregnancy. I was still holding out a bit of hope that it was all just a terrible mistake. The scan only confirmed what we already knew. My baby was implanted in my right fallopian tube. By now the rupture in my tube was more visible and my doctor was perplexed as to why I wasn't experiencing much pain. I was admitted into hospital an hour later and underwent a laparscopic salpingectomy. I lost my baby and my fallopian tube.

Affirmation

"I surrender my situation and the things that I can't control. I surrender my hurt, my pain, my anger and my grief. I allow myself to receive the support that I need right now. I trust that I am guided on my journey to healing even when the path forward isn't clear."

The Aftermath

"The mud nests of cliff swallows lined up in cracks in the canyon walls. Last summer, each would have been a perfect little clay jar with narrow-necked openings, but now their tops have been broken off by winter."

~ Kathleen Dean Moore

The surgery was fast. I woke up from it dazed to find an IV drip strapped to my arm and my husband at my bedside. It was the first time throughout the whole ordeal that I'd began to experience physical pain. I had a vague memory of being wheeled out of the operating theatre and back to my recovery ward. I recall that my husband was still sitting on the bench in the waiting area that he wasn't allowed to go beyond when they wheeled me back out after the surgery. He nervously followed as the nurse took me to the recovery room. In the spaces between dosing off and coming to, I remember being administered pain medication, my husband feeding me some sickly sweet strawberry yoghurt and him staying with me most of the evening. Each time I opened my eyes he was there, holding my hand and smiling at me. I was grateful to have him at my side. He's eyes told me that he was relieved that the surgery was over. They also held in them traces of pain and fear. I wanted very much to erase what had happened, for him not to have to carry this heartbreak behind his gentle smile. I knew that he was doing his best to be strong for me.

My husband filled me in on what the doctor reported back to him after the surgery. My right fallopian tube had been removed. They'd drained quite a lot of blood that had collected in my pelvic region as a result of the internal bleeding. The doctor seemed somewhat shocked at just how much blooded I'd lost. My remaining fallopian tube was in good condition. All in all, the surgery had gone well. The night nurses eventually asked my husband to leave as he'd stayed long after the visiting hours had ended, unnoticed. With him gone, I wrestled through the night, unable to sleep in a sterile unfamiliar place. Morning was slow to come and I couldn't wait to get out of there and to be in my own space. When I was discharged from the hospital the next morning, I breathed a huge sigh of relief. The trees were covered in raindrops and everything around us glistened in the early sunlight. There was a strange air of newness to the world that I stepped out into. After three days of good rain the earth had been cleansed and the growing sense relief and ease that washed over me brought with it the illusion that the worst was behind me.

It felt good to be home again, to return to a familiar space of sanctuary. The living room window view of my sunny autumnal garden comforted me. It looked lush, unseasonably green and so many flowers were still in bloom. Once settled, we responded to messages and made all the necessary phone calls to family and close friends, letting them know that all had gone okay, that I was well and recovering at home. I'd been prescribed really strong pain killers which meant that I slept most of the day after taking them. I felt very grateful to have a bit of peace and rest after such an eventful week. Over the next few days the people closest to us checked in, offered sympathies and support, cooked and brought us food. I was very touched by the loving presence of those who showed up to make sure that we were okay.

I didn't expect how hard things turned out to be in the weeks that followed. I'm not sure whether it was a matter of my optimism or just plain naiveté, but I'd thought that as the days rolled on I would feel better, more at peace and more able to move forward. I'd thought that I understood the nature of this sort of loss because I'd miscarried before after all, and I'd half expected that this time it would be somewhat easier for me to endure. So, I was unprepared when the dust of this frightening and painful whirlwind settled and I was left still feeling so utterly broken. There are the things that you just don't anticipate, like the fact that you still feel pregnant even when your baby is gone. My boobs were still swollen and tender, and I still felt subtle bouts of nausea. It took a few weeks for the pregnancy hormones to work their way out of my system, and almost 6 weeks for my menstrual cycle to return. It was all so confusing. Each morning I woke up expecting for it to be a better day, expecting the debilitating grief to loosen its grip a little. Yet instead, I found myself slipping deeper and deeper into a dark depression. It was completely bewildering. Yes, there were still fleeting moments of joy here and there, moments where I felt strong enough to smile or be my old and optimistic self again. Yet, for the most part, I struggled. I woke up with my heart and my body so leaden with grief that if felt as if I was sinking into the bed, my head too heavy to lift. It was difficult to get out of bed most days. Suddenly, the simple, normal, everyday life things became hard to do. My mind was scattered.

Although in reality it was still autumn, I had fallen into a winter of the soul. Each night I found myself sinking deeper into the depths of that winter, sitting bare and scarred like a naked red oak, tears rolling down my face. There was the deceptive air of lightness to it all, no leaf in sight to cover my hurt, yet, there I sat wrestling with a stone cold heaviness in my heart. Inside, I felt as dry and hard as the weathered land, frost bitten and beaten by the icy wrath of winter's breath. Bereft is the only word that came to mind as I searched for a way to articulate what I felt in my inability to reach beyond my despair. This wintry cloak with its darkness was a lonely place that cut at me with its jagged edges like a heavy dragger piercing deeper into already broken places. It felt like a desperate place where the cracks in my flesh continually shattered breath by breath, and I fell apart just a little more. Whatever hope I had of keeping myself together disappeared rapidly. Instead, I was met with the inescapable reality I'd feared most, and all I could do was bear witness as my sense of self disintegrated, my soul crushing under the weight of ever present sadness. I was there whether I liked it or not, once again with no choice other than to surrender to it. The worst had come to pass and all that was left were sherds, shattered remnants of a life I'd once imagined for myself, a life that now in this moment seemed quite impossible to ever create.

I wasn't sure why exactly experiencing this ectopic pregnancy loss was different from having a miscarriage, why it was so much more jarring and devastating. Perhaps it was the guilt and sense that I'd failed to protect my baby despite how hard they'd tried to thrive. Maybe it was that an already difficult emotional healing process now required me to come to terms with the added trauma of having had emergency surgery and now needing to face a more complicated physical recovery before I could even consider getting back to trying to conceive again. There was also the anxiety of an uncertain future, now that I had only one remaining fallopian tube and a 10% higher chance of having another ectopic pregnancy, something that was really hard to get my head around. To some degree, I wondered if perhaps it was also that the cumulative effect of my eight-year long emotionally grueling battle with subfertility and pregnancy loss hit me all at once. Either way, I was bewildered in the aftermath of my loss. Those first few weeks post-surgery in particular were quite easily the hardest I've had to live through. I honestly thought that I wouldn't be able to lift the relentless sadness that permeated every waking moment. It scared me how low I felt. I was frightened that that would be my permanent state of being, and I grappled with the idea of not knowing how to be okay again. With every passing day it became increasingly clear to me that I needed help to move through the strangely depressive space I felt lost in. I needed to do something to rescue myself. And so slowly, with the help of my husband and my support system, I began taking little steps forward to find the healing that I desperately needed.

Mending Softly Exercise

Drawing on Your Inner Strength

When you are coming to terms with your loss, grieving and navigating depression, you may not always feel as if you have the strength to get through it. Try to be kind to yourself, especially when the low moments hit and you're feeling deeply wounded and vulnerable. Acknowledge how, every day, you manage to keep breathing and to take one step after the next to keep yourself moving forward, during this difficult experience. Work on rebuilding an affirming outlook by shifting your attention to whatever makes you feel strong and resilient. Think back to a challenging situation in your life where you've had to draw on your inner strength to overcome something that felt extremely difficult at the time.

How did you find the courage to do that? What did it feel like to come through something you thought you may not survive in one piece when you got to the other side of it? And how can you connect with your inner strength and draw those qualities into your current situation?

Acknowledge the courage that you've shown in the past. Affirm your own strength. It is a reminder of your ability to navigate your current circumstances and to find a way to heal.

Part Two

The Gentle Path to Mending

The Hands of the Mender

"In the depth of winter, I finally learned that within me, there lay, an invincible summer. And, that makes me happy. For it says, that no matter how hard the world pushes against me, within me, there's something stronger…"

~ Albert Camus

I think it was the fear. The fear of an existence stuck in darkness, that is. It drove me to a place of willingness to stretch beyond the shadows and reach towards life again. That willingness is a powerful thing. I didn't know where to start exactly, but I was open to anything that would make me feel something other than pain, anything that would make me feel human or show me how to embody myself, to find joy and hope again. I wanted to remember what it was like to breathe deeply without my chest hurting so much. I wanted to remember what it was like to wake up feeling good about something in my life and to look forward to the new day despite all the uncertainty it was filled with. I just wanted to be me again. Did I have the strength to discover *"an invincible summer"* within? I needed to find out. Somewhere at the back of my mind there was also a lingering thought. I still felt that profound connection to my spirit baby even though they were no longer there in physical form. I didn't want this state of hopeless melancholy to be what the story of that baby's soul became in my life. I wanted them to mean something good. I had this idea that I couldn't give their short existence meaning if I lost myself in grief. I could only do that if I transformed my tragedy and their memory into a story of hope and healing.

In her book, Wild Grace, Kathleen Dean Moore, wrote:

"If anything grows old gracefully, it is a desert river canyon. This is a grace I would aspire to. It's an open question – how to make something beautiful of the pieces that are left after time does the slow work of the river, giving and taking, taking away."

That was what I felt called to do. I wanted to *"make something beautiful of the pieces"* that were left after what life had taken from me. Even if I couldn't see the forest from the trees while still so stuck in my grief, I was willing to try.

In this particular chapter of Wild Comfort, Dean chronicles a journey that she and her husband took canoeing through the Green River's Labyrinth Canyon. When she stumbles upon some sherds of broken pottery scattered on the cliffs where they'd set up camp for the evening, she recounts a story that her son-in-law (a conservator of ceramics) told her about how women from the Hohokam, a society of prehistoric peoples known to inhabit the North American Southwest region, traditionally mended their broken pottery. Dean wrote:

'"To mend a clay pot," Chris told me, "the Hohokam people sometimes drilled holes along the broken edges and sewed the pieces together."'

"She [the Hohokam pottery mender] threads the fibers through the holes she has drilled, aligning the cracks, pulling the ends of the cord tightly together to bind up the pot. Then she ties off the knot."

It sounds like a delicate and thoughtful process with which they skillfully pieced together these fragile fragments. Perhaps there were generations of trial and error, years of experimenting with different mediums, mending glues and pastes before these pottery menders perfected their trusted method of repairing broken vessels that must have had great significance to them. I was no skilled pottery mender like the Hohokam people were described to be. I had no method with which to mend my broken heart or to piece the remnants of my life back together. I'd reckoned that I would have to trust myself. I would have to uncover my inner 'pottery mender' by feeling my way forward intuitively, drilling and subtly threading cords of light through the holes, working carefully to rebuild with what I had. I'd have to be kind to myself too. I'd have to lean into the recesses of gentle self-compassion.

As Kathleen Dean Moore writes on about canoeing and the mending methods of ancient pottery fixers, her words seem to mirror a poignant question that kept echoing in my own heart.

"What I want to know," she writes, *"is how to take the parts that remain, the empty spaces, even the cracks, and fit them into something whole and meaningful, shaped with the kind of care that would cause a woman to spend all day drilling and stitching, drilling and stitching, trying to make strong thread by rubbing her palms against her sore thighs."*

How would I do this in my own context? I would have to find out along the way.

Affirmation

"I am my own nurturer. I heal and empower myself when I take steps to nourish my soul."

A Silent Prayer

"When the world pushes you to your knees, you're in the perfect position to pray." ~ Rumi

One sleepless night, in the midst of lightning flashes and boisterous thunder claps, as a torrent of yet more unseasonably heavy rain pelted down, I did the only thing that I could think to do when life brings you to your knees. There in my place of desperation, where the weather mirrored the gloomy currents of emotion that were beating through my veins once again, I decided to pray. However, depleted by the soul deep sobs, the strain of anxiety, fear and the unremitting sorrow that still clouded everything, I just couldn't seem to find the words. So, I asked my husband to say a prayer for us. He held me close, taking my hands in his and spoke his heart into the stormy night. The sound of his voice soothed me. The quickness of my frantically throbbing heart slowed to a calmer pace. Peace enveloped me. It was the first time in a long while that I felt held in the warm and soft spiritual essence of something greater than myself. It hadn't occurred to me until then just how abandoned I'd felt throughout navigating this challenging time. I'd switched to survival mode the moment we received the news about our ectopic pregnancy and unconsciously stopped trusting the Universe. How could I trust anything when something so precious to me had been taken away? Why did I have to go through yet another loss? Why wasn't there anyone or anything to protect me from it? I'd withdrawn into myself, exhausting every thread of strength I could muster to carry myself through. My body was hardened from tension, tired from the laboriousness of carrying my emotional load. There in prayer, I found surrender once again. I hoped that my husband did too. The sound of the rain was washing stillness into me, and washing the tension out. The surrender didn't come as a thought or as a decision. It flowed organically from the quiet space of unspoken need. And then I found my own words rising in my heart. Eyes clenched tightly, I whispered them to the ethers.

Dear Spirit,

Please show me a light out of this dark place.
Please help me find my peace.
Please guide me and help me to heal.

Mending Softly Exercise
A Prayer for Comfort

Select a prayer, an affirmation or a poem that comforts you. Choose something that feeds you spiritually, makes you feel held in love and connected to sacredness.

Bookmark it on your smartphone or print it out and keep it close.

Visit and read the soothing words that you've selected whenever you some soulful inspiration.

40 Days of Healing

"How do we move beyond it all? Is it a leap of faith, finding our way in the dark, or facing a harsh bright light?" ~ Sacred Stones, Maril Crabtree

Our prayers must have transformed something that night. The next morning, I woke up with the strong sense of what I needed do to help me move forward. I felt guided to create a "40 Days of Healing" process for myself in order to consciously take small day-to-day actions that preserved my wellbeing and helped me heal from the loss. I didn't have a concrete plan as to what this process would look like, but my internal guidance told me that bringing some sort of structure to the disorienting experience of grief would function as a stepping stone in the right direction.

So, I pinpointed a few things that I knew had helped me through challenging times in the past and ended up crafting a list of various activities that I would draw from over the period of the next 40 days. The list included a mix of healing and therapeutic practices such as holistic therapy sessions, meditation, yoga, journaling, and art therapy, as well as some simple, fun and uplifting activities that I enjoyed doing such as nature walks, gardening, reading poetry or inspirational passages from books, and things like indulging my senses with colour therapy or aromatherapy and fragrances. I didn't want to overwhelm myself with an overly structured schedule. To keep it as stress free and flexible as possible, I decided that I would choose one or two activity from the list each day and do whatever felt right in that moment. It didn't matter what it was, as long as it resonated with my soul's needs and was a positive step that I was taking to nurture and care for myself. The important thing was to hold the intention of healing in mind. How that healing manifested would become clear over time. My only responsibility during that 40-day period was to ask myself – *What is the most healing or nurturing thing that I can do for myself right now?* – and then simply do that. This simplified the process for me, especially on days where I actually only had the energy to focus on just one thing.

Although I was mindful that my grief would not miraculously evaporate, there was something cathartic about creating this space for me to work through the heaviness that I was unable to escape. Depending on the day, my healing action took the form of a therapy session or something pampering like getting a massage. Somedays I'd read poems that reflected my sadness or capture the words I was unable to express. When I felt the need for release through creative expression, I channel my emotions with watercolour paints or art therapy colouring pages. Other days, I would quieten my mind with a tea meditation or write my feelings out in my journal. At times it was the simple act of filling my house with beautiful flowers, burning natural fragrances in my diffuser or getting some new colourful linen to uplift the energy of the space. Not putting myself under the pressure of having to be okay, or at least feeling forced to pretend to be okay was freeing. Now that I had given myself permission to move slowly, flow inward and practice self-love, the balm of my mending process began to set in. Instead of wrestling with uncomfortable emotions, I was allowing myself to walk through them. I was stopping to rest when I needed it and then taking gentle steps towards healing each day.

Mending Softly Exercise

Would You Like to Create Your Own '40 Days of Healing' Process?

Gathering Your Supportive Resources: The first step to creating your own '40 Days of Healing' process is to gather the supportive resources that you will lean on during the course of your healing. What do these resources look like for you?

Here is a basic guideline of things to take into consideration:

Identify Your Emotional Support Circle. Who will you turn to for emotional support? Who will be able to guide and support you through your grieving process? You may decide to seek out a therapist, a grief counsellor, a spiritual counsellor or a holistic healing therapist depending on what resonates with you. Perhaps you would like to join an in-person or an online support group where you can be in community with people who understand what you are going through. It is also worth identifying a close friend or family member who you feel comfortable and safe turning to when you really need someone to talk to.

Identify Your 'Restorers'. What restores you? What brings you back to wholeness when you are utterly depleted? The 'restorers' that you choose are soothing things or activities. Think of them as gentle healing touchstones that resuscitate your inner life, as they help rebuild your tired body and mend your soul. Your restorers can include simple things like:

A warm bath with bath salts or bath foam
A steaming cup of chai tea
Tea meditation
Walking or grounding yourself in nature
Guided Meditations or Mindfulness exercises for inner calm and grief or anxiety relief
Art therapy and colouring
Gardening or sitting in a tranquil spot in your garden
Swimming, Yoga, Pilates or other types of gentle movement that you enjoy
Reading beautiful poetry or inspiring texts
A heartfelt conversation with a friend
A healing crystal or intention stone
A vase of your favourite flowers to uplift the energy in your home
Calming or uplifting aromatherapy oils in your diffuser to soothe your heart
Beautiful soft cotton linen
Lavender under your pillow (or lavender pillow mist to aid peaceful sleep)

These are just a few examples. Make a list of all the restorative things or activities that you love and that you feel will help aid your healing during the 40-day period. Remember that your list will be specific to you and your needs. When you are in a low place it becomes easy to turn to destructive things that only send you deeper into that negative headspace. So, it is really helpful to have soul-soothing or positive alternatives that actually aid rather than hinder your healing on hand.

Keep a Process Journal: Journaling is a simple yet powerful way to connect with our deepest feelings, thoughts and whatever is going on inside of us. It can be a therapeutic practice when it comes to working through grief and trauma. I therefore encourage you to keep a grief process journal during your 40-day period of healing. Your process journal can be an outlet where you channel your most vulnerable introspections. Make it a priority to check in with yourself to understand exactly what you are feeling and give yourself permission to feel those emotions without judgement. There is healing power in naming and looking deeper into your emotions. When you allow yourself to fully feel and process what is going on inside of you, then you are better able to understand how to look after yourself during the hard moments.

'40 Days of Healing' Process: Each day, over the course of a 40-day period, pick one or two activities from your list that you feel will help nurture you. Begin your day by asking yourself:

'What is the most healing or nurturing thing that I can do for myself right now?'

Then focus on doing that one thing for a few moments, until you feel you have gathered enough energy and strength to move forward with your day. Your needs may differ depending on the day. Somedays you may feel called to book a counseling appointment, on other days a spa day my feel like the most therapeutic thing to do. As you do just one thing, one day at a time, visualize yourself releasing the hurt and moving closer to a place of healing. The important thing is to keep it simple so that you don't feel overwhelmed by the process. Listen to what your body and your heart are asking for. Be kind and gentle with yourself. Create space for your own healing. Very importantly, if it all feels like too much to cope with, don't be afraid to reach out to someone for emotional support.

40 Days of Healing Daily Check-in Template

Day: _____

How am I feeling?

_____

What is the most healing and nurturing thing that I can do for myself right now?

_____

_____

One thing that I am grateful for today:

_____

One thing that made me feel calm and grounded today:

_____

One thing that made me feel empowered and hopeful:

_____

Allowing Rest

> *"I am learning to heed the subtle nudges of my deep feminine essence, nudges that says: "Be still for a moment. Rest, release and debrief for just a little while before the mad rush starts all over again." ~ The Fertile Moon*

'Rest and recover' was the one bit of advice that I kept getting, but couldn't seem to take on board beyond those first couple of days after returning home from the hospital. They were the last words that I wanted to hear and quite frankly seemed like the least helpful bit of guidance. I had been struggling with insomnia and was completely drained. The resultant fatigue and mind fog were affecting my wellbeing. However, I didn't want to rest. I wanted a way out of my pain. I wanted movement and other distractions. I wanted to get back to exercising and to have the sense of forward momentum as soon as possible. That movement was therapy for me. However, other than gentle nature walks (which suddenly tired me out very quickly) and subtle yoga, I wasn't able to do much of my usual physical activity since I needed to give my body a few weeks to heal after the surgery. I felt that I needed more tangible advice than just 'rest and recover'. Yet, my doctor, my naturopath and everyone else who I turned to for help all kept reiterating the same thing – *"Just take your time, focus on resting and giving yourself space to heal."*

As frustrating as it was to keep hearing this piece of guidance, a few days into my 40-day healing journey, I knew that it was what I actually needed to allow myself to do. After doing some research, I discovered that grief can indeed disrupt your sleep patterns, and that the sleep deprivation can impact negatively on your moods, immune system, anxiety levels and your cognitive ability too. Lisa Small, writer for CURE, a cancer patient support website wrote that:

"Poor sleep can go hand in hand with grieving in a downwards spiral, where physical and emotional symptoms of grief can intensify when sleep issues are not addressed. Grief can be momentary or become complicated grief over time, where advanced symptoms of grief can be emotional, physical, as well as cognitive."

Finding this kind of information showed me how necessary it was to find my balance. In addition, I realized that as people we're also conditioned to avoid our pain. So, slowing down, resting, being present with it and mindfully moving through the grief can feel incredibly uncomfortable and even threatening in a way. There is this underlying fear that facing your reality will destroy us somehow, so you run from it. You try to numb your feelings. To me, resting – not just in terms of sleeping, but also the idea of *being still* – meant sitting with the uncomfortable. I resisted doing that for as long as I could. Now, changing my approach showed me that painful though it may be to accept, in many instances the only way forward is through. Still, it felt daunting. However, I accepted that in order to move beyond the blows that had knocked the wind out of me, I had to make my peace with a situation that I couldn't change and embrace the journey, one day at a time.

When I stopped resisting, I found relief in rest. On most days it wasn't much of a choice really. My body was tired. Still emotionally drained, I struggled to rise early the way I used to and couldn't find energy to do much. I took the pressure off and let myself sleep late most mornings, getting out of bed when I felt rested. I stopped fighting the urge for things to be different than they actually were. I stopped chastising myself for being idle. Instead, my '40 days of healing' process guided me to meet myself where I was with acceptance, self-compassion and it allowed things to unfold as they needed to. Coincidently, a dear friend of mine sent me a book called 'Daring to Rest', by Karen Brody. Although I only read bits and pieces of the book and didn't follow Brody's complete programme until several months later, the little that I did read introduced me to yoga nidra, or what is also known as 'sleep yoga'. Intrigued, I searched for a few yoga nidra meditations online and incorporated them into my nightly routine. It felt as though I had some of the longest and deepest sleeps of my life. I noticed how once I let go of the self-judgement, sleep and rest felt more like a comfort than something to rail against. When I allowed myself to rest enough, my inner juices were resuscitated. Some days I had this bizarre sense that there were ghosts, or angels of healing maybe, who came at night to stitch the fragmented pieces of our lives back together as we slept. It was like healing happened deep in our slumber. We're mended softly, quietly, unnoticed to the waking eye. We wake up lighter, feeling a little newer, less burdened by the hurt of the world. Through this we find the quiet determination to move forward just a little more, no compass to guide us really, just the soft inner voice saying *'step into the unknown, onwards and upwards'*, steering towards a gentle little place called hope. And there we see so clearly that there is only one authentic path out of darkness, so we surrender to it, claiming faith in the only morsel of certainty that an uncertain future hands to us. So, we sing our heart songs on the way back to wholeness, each sherd of our shattered being melding back together, one laboured breath at a time.

Grief Release Ceremony

"Grief is sacred, and tears are liquid love streaming from the cracks of a broken heart." ~ *Zoe Clark-Coates*

A few days after our ectopic pregnancy loss, I browsed through the Audible catalogue searching for resources that I could listen to for inspiration and emotional support. I came across an audiobook by Zoe Clark-Coates called 'The Baby Loss Guide'. I spent a few days listening to it, half absentmindedly, taking in bits of guidance here and there. There was one particular thing that struck a chord with me. Clark-Coates suggested having a memorial or ceremony of sorts to honour the life of you baby as a way to bring closure for you and your partner. Open to any advice that could guide us through the mourning process, my husband and I decided that a grief release ceremony seemed like a worthwhile exercise for us to do. One evening after dinner, I gathered some candles, some flowers from the garden, our pre-conception journal and some pens to write with. We'd kept this special journal for several years. Wrapped in a deep magenta mock suede cover with a beautiful 'flower of life' motif carved on the front, its pages were filled with hope, thoughts and love letters to our future children. This journal had given us refuge, a little piece of sanctuary where we could go to let them know how much we want them in our lives. We'd share our family dreams and tell them about all the wonderful things that we are looking forward to doing together when they finally come. My husband held my hand in his as we took a few deep breaths to get centred. Doing our best not to cave under the waves of emotion that seemed to be rising to the surface, we took turns to share what we were feeling. Together, we did a short meditation to set our intentions for the ceremony – *to let go of our hurt and honour the life of our baby*. When we were ready, we each put pen to paper and individually wrote a letter to our baby.

My darling child, I wrote.

I am sorry that I couldn't protect you. Thank you for trying so hard to live. Thank you for the joy and beautiful moments you gave me for even the shortest time.

The tears flowed down my cheeks.

I am so grateful for all that you have given me. I want you to know that you are so loved and wanted. I miss you so much.

It felt strange to turn to writing on those journal pages while immersed in sadness when I was so used to turning to them for reassurance. This wasn't the type of letter that I wanted to be writing to my baby. Yet, as I let out what I was feeling and expressed what I wanted my angel baby to know, the weight of what I felt became a little lighter. This letter writing process was hard for my husband. It wasn't until that moment that he allowed himself to fully feel the magnitude of what had happened. He has always tried to be strong for me and had made nurturing me he's priority. As soon as he put his pen down, his hands covered his face and he broke down for the first time. I got up and hugged him, quietly offering comfort until he'd let it all out. It was hard not to feel responsible for his pain in that moment, or that us being in the position that we were in was all my doing. My heart crumbled. When we were ready to carry on with the ceremony, my husband and I went out onto the veranda. The air was somewhat still with only a slight hint of a breeze and the earthy scent of dew settling on the grass. We lit some floating candles and placed them in a bird bath full of cool water. I dipped my fingers into the water for a little while just to feel the coolness on my skin. There is something about water that always feels like touching peace. We gathered the garden rose and orchid flowers that I'd picked earlier on. Then, we each held a flower, focused on our intention to let go of our grief as we set them down into the water amidst the floating candles. Though it was sad to say goodbye, there was a sense of release at the same time. A few days later, when my husband and I discussed the shift we'd felt in ourselves since that evening, we both noticed how cathartic having this ceremony was for us. It gave us some closure. We'd felt a part of our emotional burden had been lifted.

Upon reflection, I came to understand why doing this grief release ceremony was important for us. I realized that so often when you experience an early pregnancy loss, whether a miscarriage or an ectopic loss, you don't always know how to process the pain and resultant grief. Couples usually don't share the exciting news about their pregnancy until they've passed the 12 week mark. So, when a pregnancy loss happens, they go through it alone, uncertain of how to give context to the devastation they may feel. There is no funeral or way of paying respects to the lost life in the traditional sense. Your pain is invisible to most, and you struggle to rationalize how you could miss a baby that you never got to meet so much. Having this ceremony thus gave us permission to own our grief, something that was very necessary in the process of letting go.

Mending Softly Exercise

Creating Your Own Grief Release Ceremony

How do you want to release your loss? Discuss the idea with your partner and identify what feels meaningful and cathartic for you both.

Would you like to light a few candles and say a prayer?

Do you want to read a poem or write a letter to your angel baby?

Or perhaps the idea of doing a blessing ceremony for your angel baby feels like something that you want to do.

Whatever it is that resonates with you, give yourself permission to do something that will help bring you a sense of closure.

Set the intention to just surrender and release.

If you need to, cry, vent and let it all out. Remember that it doesn't matter what stage of pregnancy your loss happened at, you have a right to grieve and process your emotions in a way that makes sense to you.

Learning to Focus on the Things that are Thriving

"Gardens also provide a safe haven in which to heal and renew ourselves…In a garden, we can restore our inner harmony and balance as we gain some measure of control over our lives." ~ Connie Goldman & Richard Mahler

In my ongoing pursuit of inspiration, I came across an article in which author and spiritual guru, Gabrielle Bernstein, was interviewed about the concept of 'mothering herself' and 'the power of healing her gut'. The article touched on her challenging journey to conceiving her son and included a five-step guideline that Bernstein offered to women who were also having difficulty conceiving. The first step listed was to *"Take your hands off the wheel through prayer."* Reading these words really resonated with me considering that I had done exactly that. I'd seen a notable change in myself and my healing since I had. The next step on Bernstein's list was to *"Appreciate what's thriving"*, an empowering idea that really stuck with me. Inspired by this particular tip, I began a daily practice of paying attention to all the things around me that were thriving.

"What in my life is thriving?" I'd ask myself.

"What around me is thriving right now?"

Asking these questions drew my focus to simple things that I so easily took for granted, when looking out through the lens of grief. The answers that came to me were a comfort. My marriage was thriving. My work life was thriving with amazing writing opportunities coming my way. I took pleasure in noticing the beautiful fresh flowers in my home, my treasured friendships, the vibrant colours around me, and my garden which was teeming with life too. Mostly, my attention kept going back to my garden, and as a result it became a grounding space where I found the sustenance and strength to navigate a journey that challenged me immensely. The soothing touch of soil, seeds and plants worked their therapeutic magic in my life, and continue to do so.

As a nature loving soul, I've always loved planting and growing things. From a young age the garden was a place of adventure and mystery. Some of my earliest memories are of magical days spent in my grandparent's enchanting subtropical garden where my cousin and I would be lost in play for hours. There were gigantic trees to climb, and colourful flowers or delicious juicy fruits to pick. Seeing wild animals like monkeys, frogs and exotic birds ignited our childlike excitement. We grew vegetables and both culinary and medicinal herbs. There was an orange and a banana tree orchard, along with a few macadamia nut and coffee trees at the bottom of the garden. My grandparents also kept chickens for several years too. It was the perfect place for a child to grow up in. I have a very vivid memory of one bright morning in my grandmother's kitchen when I was about 6 years old. My grand-aunt, my grandmother's younger sister, who was visiting from Australia was browsing through Gran's collection of spices when she discovered a bottle of seeds in the spice rack. In her unassuming wisdom she decided to introduce me to the joys of planting herbs from seed. We went outside, filled a small container with dark loamy soil and then planted and watered the seeds. We checked on them in the mornings to see if there was any progress. For the first three days or so, the soil was still. There were no signs of life. Then, on the fourth or fifth day, tiny little leaves had pierced their way through the sand. It was the most incredible thing I'd ever seen at the time. Throughout that school holiday, I tended to them, returning each day to water and watch them. I concluded then that plants don't grow while you're watching. I was spellbound by how much transpired when I wasn't looking. It seemed like the magic only happened at night when the stars were high and dark air rested on the soil. I remember my grandfather trying to explain something about the intelligence inside the seed telling it to grow – an essence within it that held all the knowledge of who it was and what it was supposed to do. Too young to fully understand, his words went completely over my head. But with time, the more I grew things, the more I understood what he meant.

Now in my time of need, I was reminded of the fact that there is a special kind of soul medicine that came with nurturing life, with starting cuttings and watching them take root, and with planting winter herbs in the cool wet earth after the rain. Something about the early morning garden filled my heart with its tranquility. It might be the mystery of those quiet moments where the first light returns slowly to the world, or the way the cool air settles gently on my skin like a soft kiss from a long last friend. Being in the garden brought me back to my breath. It pulled me out of my head and drew me back into my body and heart-space, so that it became an effortless exercise in mindfulness. The dew soaked grass beneath my feet was comforting. I felt like a medicine woman of old times when I gathered herbs for tea at sunrise, clipped plants and transplanted saplings in the stillness beneath the silver-blue sky before the busyness of everyday life sets in.

I discovered soul medicine in the constancy of the bees too. I made it my afternoon meditation to sit in the warm sunny 'fragrant herbal corner' of my garden and just watched the bees follow beauty, floating purposefully from flower to flower, gathering nectar from the perennial basil, borage and passion fruit daisies. I internalised their way of being by asking myself how I could mimic their approach to life –

How could I purposefully seek out the nectar of life even though I felt at my lowest?

How could I drink in the glimpses of sweetness that each daily experience offered even when I didn't know how to trust in the future?

Slowly, my heart was peeling through the layers of depression and repairing itself. As the deep breaths of herbal fragrances filled my lungs and my feet rooted down on the ground, I felt stronger, more able to put one foot in front of the other. I felt grateful for the life that surrounded me, the blue of the sky and how the earth was teaching me about the secret life of resilience. I was being reminded of how to grow through adversity and how to reach towards life once more. I'd created an opening, and this made space for the essence of life to flow back in. I was accepting that healing was a slow process and grief comes and goes in cycles. Although I wasn't sure if I would ever feel completely whole again, there was a glimpse of the light at the end of the tunnel in sight. Each day I was somewhat stunned at the fortitude I'd unearthed. I couldn't overlook the powerfully restorative role that immersing myself in nature has played in my healing journey. Tending to my garden space simultaneously allowed me to tend to and nurture my inner self and my wounds.

Weeks later, I came across a moving article by Lucy Chamberlain, who wrote about how gardening provided her with a lifeline in the midst of subfertility and failed IVF. Lucy's story resonated on various levels. It affirmed my own experiences and my belief that tending to garden life brings with it a sense of inner peace and joy that my life would be empty of otherwise. Perhaps it feeds that natural desire to create new life and the satisfaction of seeing things growing and thriving. It offers the breathing space to anchor oneself in the present moment and to feel held by the mothering energy of nature. This sometimes made me think of 'Serena Joy' in Margaret Atwood's 'The Handmaid's Tale'. In Atwood's novel, which is considered a feminist masterpiece, the garden is referred to as *"the domain of the Commander's wife [Serena Joy]"* It's an interesting coincidence that Atwood relied on this symbolism with Serena Joy, a woman who is unable to have children and who is often seen in her greenhouse nurturing and potting flowering plants in the TV series adaptation. Gardening is her therapy and I suspect that for her, as was the case with me, growing things was a fulfilling way to create and nurture life at a time when her body was unable to.

My experience with horticulture therapy, as well as that of Lucy Chamberlain's is not unique. People such as the renowned British gardening personality, Monty Don, have been vocal about how gardening has helped with his depression struggles. There is science to back it up as well. Research shows that exposure to the microbes in soil has mental health benefits, and that sunlight, fresh air and the light exercise we get while gardening also boosts our moods, relieves stress and anxiety, and aids relaxation. Interestingly, horticulture therapy has also been recognized as a treatment modality under the umbrella of psychology since the 19th century and looking back at its ancient roots supports the fact that this is a time proven practice. Early documents and literature tell us that the first known healing gardens date back to approximately 10,000 years ago, in 2000 BC in Mesopotamia. Gardens were used for their aesthetic and therapeutic function in ancient Chinese and Japanese culture. Healing gardens were also a prominent feature in many monasteries who offered curative treatments to surrounding communities during the middle ages in Europe. In more recent times, the rehabilitative care of hospitalized war veterans in the 1940's/50's facilitated the expansion and acceptance of horticulture therapy as a remedial practice. It is applied quite successfully as a therapy for children, the elderly, Alzheimer's patients and anorexia patients in various treatment facilities around the world, engaging patients in tactile and sensory activities that improve their sense of wellbeing.

"When I see my garden flourish, I regain my resilience, my balanced perspective, and my peace of mind. The garden has proven itself as my best medicine, my partner in recovery and restoration. Through gardening, I can always find my way back into a healthy resonance and a satisfying harmony with the world."

~ Connie Goldman & Richard Mahler

Writing Prompt

Explore the following questions in your process journal:

What is thriving in your life right now?

If you look around you, what or who is thriving in your environment?

How can you focus your attention on and appreciate the things that are working well in your life?

Mending Softly Exercise

Creating Your Own Therapeutic Gardening Practice

Does the idea of gardening therapy resonate with you? If it's something that you would like to explore, then it's worth looking for a horticulture therapy support group in your area. If you are unable to find one, then here are some ideas to help you create your own healing gardening practice:

Make your gardening time your self-care: Use your time in the garden as an opportunity to de-stress and release anxiety. Take deep breaths of fresh air and enjoy the relaxing vibrations of your natural space. Enjoy the feel of the soil. Grow plants that are meaningful to you – edible plants, your favourite flowers and uplifting colours. If you enjoy fresh fragrances, then consider creating a fragrant herbal garden to revel in their healing scents and reap their aromatherapy benefits. Herbs like rosemary, thyme, perennial basil, lemon verbena and scented geraniums are hardy and beautifully fragrant. Investigate growing plants that attract bees, butterflies and birds as this is a good way of inviting garden life and vibrant energy into your space. Take time to watch things grow and appreciate your space. It is so rewarding knowing that not only are you tending to your garden, but you are nurturing your wellbeing and mending your heart as well.

Create a Fertility Garden Meditation Corner: Create a space in your garden where you can sit, relax, enjoy the sun and watch the activity in your lively garden unfold. Sit in quiet contemplation, sip some tea, breathe mindfully and observe the simplicity of life. Take time to journal or do a calming meditation to release tension and anxiety. Notice any messages or lessons that your natural surround may be teaching you. Focus on the things that are thriving. Observe the creative power of nature. Draw it all in, reminding yourself of your own creative power to renew your energy, to heal and to create new life in the same way.

Bring Nature into Your Home: Get some indoor plants and flowers. Choose plants that are low maintenance, hardy and easy to tend to. Try your hand at keeping some herbs on a sunny kitchen windowsill so that you can pick them easily and use them while cooking. Get some pretty flowering bulbs, they always make beautiful and uplifting table centrepieces and liven up dreary corners. Put your indoor plants in places where you will be able to see and appreciate their beauty as they grow. Also consider putting a bird bath or feeder outside a sunny window where you can sit indoors and observe the sprightly birds at play.

The Second Wave: Dealing with PTSD and Anxiety

"We emerge into the light not by denying our pain, but by walking through it." ~ *Joan Borysenko*

One never full understands how layered trauma is until you are walking through the ring of fire gasping in confusion under the pressure of its deceptive and suffocating hold. It takes you by surprise. One moment you let your guard down, so sure that you have reached the other side of a seemingly unbearable experience, and the next you're knocked back down to the floor. All the progress that you thought you'd made quickly becomes a mere figment of your imagination and you feel as though suddenly you are right back to square one.

Everything seemed to be going well. I went for my follow up appointment, my body had healed and since enough time had passed, my husband and I were given the all-clear to start trying to conceive again. It was a relief to be able to move on. Finally, there was some forward momentum on our path to parenthood. However, almost as soon as I readied myself to begin the conception journey, I was overcome by bouts of anxiety and unexpected panic attacks. At first it felt misplaced, sudden and came seemingly from nowhere because I couldn't pinpoint it to anything specific. Suddenly, ordinary situations felt overwhelmingly stressful. My body would shut down because I couldn't breathe properly. It was as if my body had become a hostile environment and I had an inexplicable urge to escape it. It took me several weeks to recognize that what I was experiencing was actually some degree of post-traumatic stress disorder, most likely triggered when my husband and I got back to trying to conceive. This period quickly turned into a frustrating few months. It took me great effort to calm my mind and not feel disempowered by what seemed like yet another roadblock. It was strange territory to navigate. It felt unexpected because I hadn't grappled with PTSD after any of my previous miscarriages, so I struggled to understand why it was happening to me this time, especially when I had put in a lot of work to heal after my loss. As I took steps to find the necessary emotional support, I discovered that statistics in some countries show that 1 in 6 women who suffer a pregnancy loss experience PTSD afterwards. Through self-examination I personally came to realise that when you've experienced pregnancy loss more than once it becomes difficult to trust in your body's ability to conceive and carry a healthy pregnancy to term. There is always the fear that it will happen again. Every twitch, sensation or dull ache becomes a trigger. In my case, this time around I had zero pain or symptoms of an ectopic pregnancy ahead of my first scan. I'd thought that my days of pregnancy loss were behind me because everything was fine, until it wasn't. It felt as though I'd been lulled into a false sense of security before being slapped in the face with an unwelcome rude awakening. This made it difficult to trust that I was actually safe or healthy. I felt more at ease during a cycle where I knew I wasn't trying to conceive as compared to a month when I knew there was a possibility of being pregnant. It became a catch-22, as I feared both not being able to get pregnant as well as the possibility of getting pregnant only to experience another loss at the same time. I'd struggled with intimacy for fear that if I got pregnant again too soon it would end up being another ectopic pregnancy. I knew of women in the ectopic recovery groups that I belonged to who had two or even three consecutive ectopic pregnancies. On the flipside, I also knew women who'd gone on to quickly conceive and have a healthy pregnancy after their ectopic. But I guess that once you've experienced the worst case scenario the mind always goes to that place, expecting that it will happen again, fearful of reliving the trauma, only not being able to survive it all this time. And so you remain in fight-or-flight mode – tense, anxious and mistrusting. To your post-trauma afflicted mind the world is a dangerous place and so the panic attacks start to take hold.

Psychotherapist and author, Joanna Flemons (LCSW, CPC), sheds some light on the topic in her book, 'Infertility and PTSD – The Uncharted Storm'. Flemons says that *"...infertility, ectopic pregnancy, recurrent pregnancy loss, stillbirth and other facets of this arduous journey can result in PTSD symptoms. Facing infertility in the present while regulating intrusive PTSD symptoms from past trauma and loss is an enormous challenge."*

She goes further to say that: *"The helplessness from the loss of control over your body is profound. The recurring loss can create the potential for new trauma and PTSD."*

Reading Flemons' book helped put my own experiences into context and to understand that my anxiety was an understandable reaction to the trauma and loss that I had experienced. In the initial stages when the panic attacks began, I reached out to women in one of the ectopic recovery support groups to get an idea of whether anyone else went through something similar. Several women were kind enough to respond and share their stories with me, many of whom shared that they felt that the PSTD along with the resultant anxiety never fully goes away, as in their case it persisted even after having a healthy pregnancy. Some admitted that they didn't realize that this was what was going on with them and were relieved to learn that they weren't alone in their struggle. It was a little scary for me to hear some of these stories, but it also showed me how important it was to address the issues that lie beneath the surface, reach out for emotional assistance when necessary, and to have a good support system to lean on. It reinforced the importance of having these difficult discussions in community so that women who are struggling feel less isolated as well.

It was important to me that I be in as grounded and healthy a space as possible when I was ready to conceive again. I was so conscious of the kind of energy I wanted to invite my baby into. I therefore took the decision to give myself more time to understand what my triggers were and to work through them. Along with doing the inner emotional work and releasing my physical tension, working at rebuilding my trust in my body, as well as my confidence in my ability to conceive and have a healthy full-term pregnancy became a key focus. I had my work cut out for me, but I was willing to do what I needed to in order to feel more balanced and whole. Once again I would have reach deep into the medicine bag of my inner nurturer. I'd have to get reacquainted with the artful skills of the shamanic 'pottery mender' within and find ways to put her mending abilities to use. She had been kind to me, this proverbial 'pottery mender', quietly teaching how to feel human again, and the threads of light that she guided me to in her wisdom were stitching my heart's sherds back together tightly so that I felt a lot more complete with the passage of time. I trusted her more, now. My self-imposed '40 days of healing' journey had shown me how to align the cracks, how to smooth the jaggered edges, piece by piece. I found healing in simplicity, stillness, nature and creativity. Joanna Flemons' book also offered some really valuable guidance on coping with PTSD. She highlighted that:

"During infertility and PTSD, it is important to develop a regular routine of activities that strengthen your mind to increase body health, while also reducing anxiety and stress. Mind-body practices can include meditation and acupuncture...These practices allow you to separate and disconnect from stimuli and outside stress that might otherwise vie for your attention."

I took this on board when it came to my self-care and finding practical solutions. The unanticipated PTSD added a complicated layer to the process, yet even so, although it now seemed that I was only halfway there I knew that I was in good hands.

Mending Softly Exercise

Mini – Meditations to Ground You

[1] **"I am Calm" Breathing Meditation:** Bring your hands to your heart center. Take a deep breath in and out. Be present in your body.

Take a few more deep breaths. As you do, inhale peace and calm, exhale fear and anxiety.

Repeat for a minute or two until you feel ready to move forward in a more grounded energy space.

[2] **"I am Safe" Mini – Meditation:** Lay your back comfortably against the ground. Place one hand over your heart and the other over your belly. Take a few long deep breaths in and out, feeling your belly rise and fall as you do. Notice how your body is lovingly supported by the earth beneath you. Let go of your fears and allow yourself to feel held in a blanket of protective energy.

As you inhale, say: "I am safe and supported."

Exhale, and say: "I am lovingly protected from all harm."

[3] **"I am Grounded" Mini – Meditation:** Feel your feet against the earth, soles resting firmly on the ground. Sense the stable and supportive energy of the earth beneath you and draw this energy up into your body. Feel yourself grounding, as you release any anxiety and tension from your body.

Inhale and say: "I am rooted on sacred ground."

Exhale and say: "I am steady and unmoved by the chaos around me."

Healing the Trauma

"In this house of clay and water, my heart lies in ruin without you. Dear soul, please enter this house, so I can begin to rebuild." ~ Rumi

"If you knew yourself for even one moment," says Rumi, the renowned Sufi poet, *"if you could just glimpse your most beautiful face, maybe you wouldn't slumber so deeply in that house of clay."* The poem goes on as follows:

"Why not move into your house of joy and shine into every crevice!

For you are the secret Treasure-bearer, and always have been.

Didn't you know?"

But what happens when that 'house of clay' no longer feels comfortable or like a place of joy? When the shock of trauma or tragedy shakes us, sometimes little bits of our inner essence splinter off and we desert ourselves. We don't know how to be in our bodies or how to embody who we once were. The shattering can numb your soul, cause you to disassociate from yourself and leave you feeling like a ghost floating somewhere outside of yourself, detached and looking into life from the periphery. You are a vagrant, lost to the world in some ways and unsure of how to come back home to yourself.

In my healing, I became not just a proverbial pottery mender to my own soul, but also a gatherer, roaming invisible plains retrieving lost and broken parts of myself, calling them back home. I had to get very still to relearn how to be comfortable with the empty spaces that my loss had left behind. Fortunately for me, I had some help to guide and restore me back to myself.

There are profound moments in life where the Universe has surprised me, instants when blessings have shown up to rescue me and I have felt so lovingly supported in the face of turmoil. Perhaps when I call out for help in desperation I only half expect it to arrive, because often I am in disbelief when I am led to exactly where and what I needed. I am shaken, in awe of how perfectly it all happened to 'just fall into place'. I felt that one morning at the end of an early Saturday aerial yoga class, when a really kind and empathic person happened to refer me to a holistic healing therapist. The said healer was in town for a few weeks and would be offering one-on-one sessions at the studio's therapy room while she was around. The timing could not have been more perfect considering that my struggles with anxiety and panic attacks were at their peak. She'd also had lots of experience and success in assisting women who had trouble conceiving. I jumped at the opportunity and booked a session with her for the soonest available appointment date.

When I walked into the warm therapy room a week later, the mid-morning sunshine was streaming in, creating a bright and airy atmosphere. I wasn't sure what to expect, but I was hopeful. The holistic therapist was a lovely cheerful woman with a very calming presence. She immediately put me at ease as she told me a bit about her life, her years of healing experience, the different courses that she studied, her travels and how she walked the Camino in her 60s. Our session included a variety of different healing modalities. She worked on balancing and clearing my energetic and emotional blocks. She was really perceptive and accurate in the things that she picked up about me. When we did some 'body sensing' and progressive relaxation therapy, I was completely shocked by how much tension my body was unconsciously holding on to. This was how my body was responding to the trauma. I noticed how stiff and tight my jaw was from all the stress and anxiety. My shoulders, back and inner thigh muscles were rock hard too. I hadn't realized just how much I actually needed the body work. The muscle relaxation exercises worked wonders in helping me release the tension and blocks from my body. We talked through my emotions and she offered me loads of valuable guidance and coping tools. Each session ended with calming music and a guided meditation specifically tailored to whatever issue I was addressing on the day. I felt a massive weight being lifted and walked out of there feeling relaxed and so much lighter.

My sessions with the healer were an important catalyst. Several years earlier, when I studied a course in Relaxation Therapy, I'd learnt so many useful de-stress, mindfulness and anxiety relief techniques that I'd forgotten about. Now, with the help of this holistic therapist, I was being reminded of how to use these coping tools to alleviate the physical, mental and emotional stress that was crippling me. It was the nudge that I needed, and incorporating these resilience-building techniques into my self-care practices was immensely helpful in dealing with my trauma. As a Reiki practitioner myself, I started to do more self-healing energy work on myself in-between sessions. Again, the yoga nidra meditations were a massive help. I also resumed the womb connection meditations that I had been doing regularly in the months before I fell pregnant. In her book, 'Yes You Can Get Pregnant', the author Aimee E Raupp, says that in Traditional Chinese Medicine the uterus is referred to as the *'child's palace'*. Raupp offered a great affirmation that quickly became part of my daily womb connection practice while I was preparing to conceive. The affirmation is as follows:

"Dear Uterus, you are the palace of my child and I believe in you. I send you love and joy. You are a beautiful palace, brimming with fertility, and I fully believe in your ability to get pregnant."

I'd loved the good feelings that this affirmation filled me with whenever I placed my hands on my belly and recited it. I'd found some really powerful womb meditations in Tami Lee Kent's books, 'Wild Feminine' and 'Mothering From Your Center' too. Kent shares a good amount of valuable information about pelvic care and forming a healthy relationship with an area of our bodies that we are often disengaged from. Putting her guidance and feminine healing wisdom to use had been a hugely beneficial part of my fertility journey. Most evenings before bed I would lie down with my hands on my lower abdomen, spending love and positive energy into my womb space. I'd visualize clearing any stagnant energy and I'd focus on creating a welcoming home to invite my baby into. This practice allowed me to feel so connected to my baby during those short-lived weeks in early pregnancy. However, since the ectopic pregnancy and the surgery, I had stopped. As one would imagine, the trauma led me to disassociate from my womb space. Fortunately, the holistic healer had helped me rekindle my connection to my womb. I did meditations to release the pain and trauma that I'd being storing in this space. It felt strange. For the first time the reality of having had a part of my reproductive organs removed registered properly in my mind. It was a bizarre thing to wrap my head around when I was visualizing my womb space which now had one fallopian tube missing. It brought up mixed emotions – fear, sorrow, hurt and anger. I felt defective. Since my focus had been completely on grieving the loss of my baby, I hadn't actually come to terms with the physical changes I'd suffered as a consequence of the ectopic pregnancy and the emotional impact thereof. The loss of this body part had been virtually invisible and thinking about its implications for my future fertility made me fearful. As a result, I didn't know how to interact with this area of my body when a piece of it had been physically taken from me. Now that I'd become more aware of it, I would have to keep finding ways to process and make peace with the physical trauma that my body had undergone. I was ready to let it go and reclaim my relationship with both my physical self and my womb.

Participating in physical activities that I loved became a significant part of rebuilding my trust and confidence in my body. For the most part, aerial yoga in particular played a significant role in helping me find the balance and healing that I desperately needed. Not only was it a great physical outlet for me considering that exercise is an effective way to alleviate anxiety, but it also fed me emotionally from the very first moment I got into the hammock. I remember my first aerial yoga class quite vividly. I sat in lotus position beneath the bright purple hammock, nervous and not sure what to expect. There was something soothing about the way the radiant afternoon light poured into the movement studio. It felt nostalgic, reminding me of those lazy Saturdays in my teens when the world felt exciting and full of new possibilities. I'd seen several beautiful pictures and snippets of videos with women gracefully suspended in their acrobatic poses. While I'd liked the idea of it, I wasn't quite sure how I would ever be able to do any of those things. In fact, I was completely intimidated at the prospect of what was about to unfold.

"What have you gotten yourself into now?" I wondered quietly.

However, I knew that I was there because needed to try new things. I was looking for ways to reignite my passion for life at a time when so much in it felt tainted by subfertility and recurrent pregnancy loss. So, the idea of aerial yoga was a welcome step away from my everyday reality, a refreshing opportunity to experience something different. The instructor, a lovely, warm and gentle woman who I quickly grew to love, began by guiding us through a brief meditation to set our intentions for the class. We perused the beginner's instruction manual to get acquainted with the basics of aerial yoga. From there she eased into the practice, starting first with slow easy stretches that allowed us to familiarize ourselves with the hammock. Then we worked our way through to more complex yoga asanas and inverted poses – basically, the intimidating stuff that I'd been afraid of. Each step of the way I found myself thinking:

"Nope, there's absolutely no way I could possibly do that move!"

And each time, my instructor would gently guide me through the movement and encourage me to try it one or two more times until I got the hang of it before we moved on to the next thing. I was stunned to find myself doing inverted monkey poses, shoulder stands, tumbling in and out of the hammock and flying. I left that introductory workshop feeling so heartened by my achievement. The following week I returned to the movement studio and began attending regular classes. I fell deeply in love with the sense of freedom that doing aerial yoga gave me. It felt amazing to achieve something I didn't think I could at the outset. The more I strengthened my core and saw myself grow from class to class, then the easier it became for me to trust my body and its many capabilities.

I returned to the movement studio about eight weeks after my ectopic pregnancy loss, when I was able to resume with more strenuous physical activities. Naturally, I'd lost confidence in myself and it was really difficult to trust in my body's ability to function properly after all that had happened. Even so, aerial yoga welcomed me back like a long last friend. I slowly eased back into the practice, reacquainting myself with gentle stretches and deep breaths.

There was something about the strength of the hammock fabric and the way that it held my weight through every yoga pose that was reassuring, a constant that reminded me that there were some things that could be relied upon even when my world was in a state of chaos. Once again, it helped me to rebuild my relationship with my body. It was a vehicle for re-establishing the trust that was lost, and a reliable resilience building tool when it came to managing my PTSD and anxiety symptoms. This practice liberated me from the things that weighed me down. The more I leaned into aerial yoga, the more it gave me the courage to keep challenging myself. In time, it peeled away more layers to show me I was stronger than I'd thought I was. In an article published by Yoga Journal, about how yoga can help people with PTSD, a mindfulness based psychotherapist who uses yoga in her trauma recovery programmes highlighted that yoga *"helps disengage the sympathetic (fight--or-flight) response, which is in overdrive when a person struggles with post--traumatic stress."* The psychotherapist, Kayla Bettis – Weber, added that *"PTSD treatment focuses strongly on engaging the parasympathetic nervous system, which corresponds to states of calm, digestion, and orientation to time and space."* The article suggests that Yin and Hatha Yoga *"are particularly suitable for trauma survivors, thanks in part to the breath-work and compassionate observation of the internal and physical experience."* Bettis–Weber concludes that *"Eventually, this skill translates into un-attaching from intense emotional and physical waves of trauma symptoms so that you witness the experience rather than feel fear or shame."*

If that wasn't enough, I also discovered something that was absolutely mind-blowing. I had anticipated that it would be harder to get pregnant with just one fallopian tube, but in actual fact my situation wasn't as dire as I had thought. As it turned out, the remaining fallopian tube is still able to float over to the ovary on the other side where the tube has been removed to collect a mature egg should you ovulate from that side. The single fallopian tube is thus able to stand in for the tube that is no longer there. Learning this showed me just how miraculous the body is. Although I still have no guarantee as to how my fertility journey will end, it was a reassuring piece of information to come by. How could I not trust in its divine intelligence now?

Adding to that, one of the ladies in the ectopic pregnancy support group reminded me of the difference that shifting your mindset in a positive direction can make. She pointed out that although I now had a 10% chance of having another ectopic, there was also a 90% chance that the baby will implant in the right place and I would have a healthy normal pregnancy next time round. Her comment put things into perspective for me. As mentioned, a lot of my stress and anxiety stemmed from the fear of that 10% chance of it happening again. So, her comment motivated me to focus on the other 90% instead. Each time I felt the anxiety of what could go wrong rising, I would try to shift my attention to what could go right. I visualized a positive outcome and worked with positive affirmations to focus on the beautiful possibilities of the pregnancy and motherhood I wanted to experience. It was a great way to put my mind at ease.

Affirmation

"My body is a safe place. I am grounded and secure. When I focus on the soothing rhythm of my breath, then I open up a peaceful pathway to inner wellbeing and calm."

Mending Softly Exercise

Four Supportive Self-Care Practices to Consider when Dealing with Post-Trauma Stress and Anxiety

Mindfulness Practices and Progressive Relaxation Therapy: Progressive relaxation therapy is a really simple way to relax the body and calm the mind. It involves tensing and relaxing all the muscles in your body one section at a time. Stress and anxiety cause our muscles to tighten and our bodies to tense up. So, when you release tension from your body and allow your muscles to relax completely, you start to shift out of that anxiety riddled fight or flight mode. Your mind eases and feels safer. In addition, breathing exercises are another deep relaxation technique that works well in conjunction with progressive muscle relaxation. If you've had an anxiety attack then you probably know that struggling to breathe is one of the first symptoms you pick up on. The quickest way back to presence is to focus on your breath. The rhythm of your breath is calming. It draws your attention away from upsetting distractions and back into the moment. At any moment when you become self-aware during an overwhelming moment, breathe deeply and allow yourself to be. Other things that have also been helpful to me personally include going for massages, acupuncture and reflexology.

Rebuilding Body Confidence and Trust: What kinds of activities help you to reconnect with your body? Perhaps for you it's something like aerobics, running, yoga, dancing, Pilates, walking or swimming. It's worth finding an activity that you can enjoy regularly to rebuild a positive relationship with your body. Do these physical activities a few times a week. Keep the intention of reestablishing trust in your body in mind. Remember to be kind and patient with yourself and your body in the process. If physical activity is not appealing to you, then consider creating a body love practice where you focus on expressing gratitude for your body and work on self-acceptance.

Mindset and Positive Affirmations: Shift your focus away from self-judgement and reframe the negative thoughts that destroy your sense of self-worth and body confidence. How can you look at your situation or yourself differently? How can you be self-compassionate instead of harshly critical? Take note of your limiting beliefs and then work on replacing those toxic thoughts with nurturing and empowering ones. Positive affirmations and inspirational oracle cards provide a wonderful daily focus to meditate on so that you start to reframe your thinking. It's so easy to come down hard on yourself for not getting things 'right', not being 'good enough', etc. These are the very moments when you need to be kind to yourself.

Art Therapy: Similar to journaling, art therapy is a creative self-examination and self-expression tool. In recent years, art therapy has proven to be an effective form of stress relief. The rise in popularity of adult colouring books is testament to just how effective a tool it is when it comes to calming the mind and engaging your playful creative side. It's so therapeutic to just disconnect from everything and play around with watercolors or do some colouring. The colours you choose always tell a story about your emotions and unspoken thoughts. So, it's a lighthearted way to just let it all out.

Healing as a Couple

"There's nothing more beautiful then the way the ocean refuses to stop kissing the shoreline, no matter how many times it's sent away." ~ *Sarah Kay*

For all the adversities that life has dealt me, I am ever grateful for the man who chose to love me through it all. He is the beautiful soft place of comfort where I know I will always land safely no matter how hard I fall. I give thanks every day that we found our way to one another. I am grateful that in the 20 years that we've known one another and in the 11+ years that we've been married, our love and affection for one another has grown deeper and stronger. When people learn of our fertility story, the losses and the difficulty we've had then many questions tend to follow. A frequent one tends to be:

"How is your marriage going to survive subfertility?"

Our answer is that we've always been mindful of the fact that subfertility is not a problem within our relationship, but rather a life challenge that we face together as a couple.

Yes, as a couple dealing with fertility struggles, you do fall into rough patches. Sometimes the stress or emotional turmoil that comes with the territory puts strain on you as individuals and on your relationship too. Sometimes you withdraw from one another and other times the anger or frustration that you feel makes it tempting to lash out at each other. Rough patches are normal in any relationship regardless of what you are facing. At the end of the day, you try your best to find a healthy balance between a place of peace and the tug and pull of your struggle. I'll re-iterate that I believe that a healthy and loving relationship is the foundation that we'll build our one-day family on. This means that it's so important to create a supportive environment in which your love and marriage can continue to flourish despite the testing times you may be living through together.

There is a poem by Margaret Atwood, called 'Habitation', that offers a very interesting depiction of marriage. In the opening lines of the poem, Atwood tells us that:

"*Marriage is not*
a house or even a tent
it is before that, and colder:
the edge of the forest, the edge
of the desert"

At first glance, I felt that this was a pretty bleak depiction of marriage. It seemed strange to compare it to a cold place on the *'edge of a forest'*. However, I realized that she is reminding us that marriage, like any relationship, isn't always easy. She goes on to tell us that marriage is:

"the edge of the receding glacier
where painfully and with wonder
at having survived even
this far

we are learning to make fire"

The sentiment of this poem is completely transformed by its last line.

"We are learning to make fire," she writes.

Isn't this exactly what we do in marriage? We are working at keeping the hearth burning at our center, each of us bringing our own logs to the fire, our personal effort and contribution to sustaining it's warmth through darkness and through the calm sunny afternoons of midsummer. We come together around our hearth to celebrate our love for one another when times are good. We work at keeping that fire going through the bitterness of our coldest winters. That fire is where we bake our clay pots and mend our broken sherds. That nurturant fire offers us comfort and hope at times when we don't know how to find the strength to carry on, when we don't know if we'll ever be able to move forward without falling apart. And when we do fall apart, we find ourselves comforted in the loving embrace of its brilliant glow. At times it is the only constant in a hostile world where nothing else makes sense.

When it comes to grieving a pregnancy loss and healing together as a couple, it has been important for us to remember that we all respond to challenging life events differently. We each process loss differently and work through grief in our own way. When I had an early miscarriage a few years ago, I was devastated. Yet, on the surface it appeared to me as though my husband was un-phased by what had happened. I struggled to understand why it didn't seem to affect him the way it affected me, and I took it all very personally. On a really bad day where I was feeling very triggered, I snapped and lashed out at him. My reaction took him by surprise. However, it also opened the door to an honest conversation about what we were both feeling and how our individual coping mechanisms were playing out. When my husband didn't react to our loss in the same way that I did, I took it as him expecting the pregnancy to fail, something that made me feel that he didn't have faith in my ability to carry to term. That thought made me feel like even more of a failure. In reality, that wasn't the case at all. By talking things out, I discovered that my husband's modus operandi is always to put my wellbeing first. In this case he felt that meant putting his own feelings aside to be strong for us and to nurture me. It was a constructive conversation for us both, because it gave us a better understanding of one another. We found a middle ground where we could both communicate openly and create a safe space for each other to work through our emotions and grief together. Having a safe space is incredibly important, since no one feels comfortable expressing themselves if they know that they're going to be judged. The understanding that we developed in that particular instance laid the groundwork for how to deal with our ectopic pregnancy loss in a way that was more sensitive to one another. We recognized each other's various methods of coping with grief and were thus able to offer support or space accordingly.

Nurturing your relationship looks different for everyone, since just as we all grieve differently, our needs, communication styles and love languages also vary from person to person. So, I believe that it is important for you to explore and find out what resonates with you as a couple. In my personal experience, there are two things that I feel have played a significant role in strengthening my relationship with my husband as we have navigated our fertility and pregnancy loss journey – those are creating space for connection outside of the pressures of fertility concerns or other challenges, and good communication.

Several years ago, while on holiday on the West Coast, my husband and I spent the day visiting old friends who were excited to introduce us to their toddler (after struggling to have a baby for a while). We had a beautiful day catching up and it was heart-warming to see their joy. During the course of the day our conversations shifted to various different topics until it eventually turned to the one bit of marriage advice that they felt really helped strengthen their relationship during their struggles. It was something that they had learned when they attended a marriage reboot retreat of sorts. They set up two chairs in one corner of their living room, and each day when they got home from work, before attending to household chores or anything else, they would go sit down in their chairs and have a conversation about their day. Those chairs became their sacred space, a place where they could just disconnect from the world, daily demands and the various roles they had to play, and just be present with one another.

A couple of years later, when our own fertility journey and the emotional fallout of pregnancy loss began to take its toll on us, we remembered their story and decided to explore how we could create our own space for connection. We settled on the idea of what we call our 'candlelight breakfasts'. We loved the idea of bringing a touch of romance to the ordinary. Weekday evenings were tricky as our work hours can be erratic, but our mornings tend to be calm. We usually do an 8km morning walk at sunrise and then come home to have breakfast before getting on with the day's work. We figured that this would be the best time of day to create a ritual that offers us the opportunity to be present, connect, communicate and tend to our relationship.

One could say that by doing so, we created a kind of sacred space for ourselves. Each morning, we'd light a candle at our little dining table and sit down to breakfast together. During this time we were just two people spending quality time together, so we'd set our cellphones aside and didn't discuss anything fertility related. Instead, we'd discuss our goals and intentions for the day, what we're feeling, what we're grateful for or inspired by. And then one thing that I considered very significant is that we made a point of asking the question:

How can I support you?

We didn't always know how to ask for support or address our needs. Learning to do so taught us not just to take better care of ourselves, but to take better care of each other too. It reinforced my belief that keeping the lines of communication open is key in any relationship. Knowing how to support each other, whether soothing one another's pain, sharing chores, offering inspiration or celebrating joys and successes, helps to cement the bond that your relationship is founded on. It showed us that listening to each other and following through on the agreements that we make are an important part of that cycle of connection and communication as well. Although it felt a bit silly at first, our candlelight breakfast ritual quickly become a valuable tool for fostering a sense of togetherness so that we moved through the rest of the day feeling supported. This became a cherished practice in the aftermath of our ectopic pregnancy loss, one that made me deeply appreciative to have tools that we could lean on in order to maintain our closeness even in a time of emotional distress. Around three months after our loss, the inevitable happened. My husband was retrenched from his job as the company he worked for liquidated. This disrupted our lives and jolted us into a place of even greater uncertainty. We had to make a conscious effort to remain positive and seek out creative solutions as we worked to regain our stability. Fear around unexpected changes can easily upset the balance within a relationship. Knowing that the challenges that we faced could become all-consuming if we focused solely on them, we recognized that the situation required us to be mindful and to keep practicing what we knew was working for us. When we were fearful, we were honest about it and did whatever we could to find solutions and new income generating opportunities. It was important to me to devote my energy constructively, keep a positive mindset and to be someone to lean on as my husband found the courage to start he's own business. We didn't want to waste our energy on negativity and fear-based conflict. Soon enough, our efforts paid off, things worked themselves out and once again we felt we'd laid another solid brick in the foundation of our relationship despite the circumstances we'd faced.

Throughout it all, I felt comforted in just surrendering to and enjoying the little things that made us 'us'. Not just the candlelight breakfast ritual, but also the familiar things that we've done together for many years now. Like how we lie in bed some nights, listening to jazz and reading poetry or interesting essays to one another, and then discuss our insights, our perspectives on life and which words and bits of prose moved us. Or like how we often hold hands on our morning nature walk, talk about our dreams and sit down for a quiet moment to meditate together at the water's edge when we reach the halfway point of our walk. Those relaxed moments, whether on holiday or at home, when we are disconnected from the world and simply enjoying the pleasure of one another's company feel so real, so 'us'. They take the pressure off and offer us freedom from life's challenges where we can simply be two lovers living and dreaming together. Those moments become a place where we meet each other halfway, without hassle. In difficult times they became like temper, strengthening the clay that we were molding, shaping and building together. Healthy communication and methods of cultivating closeness assisted us, especially during the period when I was dealing with PTSD and struggled with physical intimacy. The non-physical connection was the first step in reestablishing my sense of safety and security so that we could find a comfortable path back to one another. Regardless of how our lives evolve, I do hope that this is something that we'll continue to do for years to come. I feel that there are no perfect lives or marriages, but I do believe that there are happy ones. Indeed, challenges always arise as a natural part of life. The real test, however, is in how we choose to navigate our way through them.

Writing Prompt

Nurturing Your Relationship

What does nurturing your relationship and creating space for connection or communication look like for you?

How can you step outside of your fertility concerns and reconnect with your partner, nurture your bond with one another and have care-free fun together?

What are your needs? What would make you feel more supported?

What are your partner's needs? Where can you offer them support?

How can you create space for dialogue and ensure that you communicate openly and effectively with each other?

How can you get better at listening to one another?

Mending Softly Exercise

Three Soulful Ways to Foster Connection

Bedtime Poetry Sessions: Get a collection of love-themed poetry. Choose one or two evenings that work best for you. When you go to bed on those nights, take turns to each read one of your favourite love poems to one another. Share what you love about the poem. Discuss the themes, the lines that move you and emotions their words stir in you. Explore new poems together each week and remember to keep it light and love-filled. Not everyone is able to express what they feel, so poetry is a great way to share the things that you may be unable to say. (**If poetry is not your thing, then substitute it with beautiful love songs that will help you connect deeper with one another.**)

Sensual Massage: Massage can be a soothing and pleasurable sensual experience. It's a great way to encourage intimacy. Set aside some quiet time to be together. Play gentle music. Light some candles. If you have an aromatherapy diffuser or oil burner, then choose some calming scents to aid relaxation. Have some warming sensual oils or a massage cream on hand, get comfortable and then take turns giving and receiving massages to one another. Take deep breaths, release your tension, enjoy the sensual touch and the chance to nurture a physical connection with your partner.

Heart Space Meditation: Sit down comfortably with a cushion on the floor or a bed with your partner. Facing one another, look into each other's eyes. Hold hands or let your palms touch. Take a few deep breaths in and out, relaxing into one another's presence. Breathe into your heart space, connecting with the vibration of love. Visualise loving energy pouring out from your heart and flowing into your partner's as you keep breathing, in and out. Think of the ways in which you like to express your love for them, how happy this makes them feel and continue to send them loving energy for a few moments. Now shift your attention to receiving the out pouring of love from your partner's heart space. Allow yourself to receive. Think of your favourite romantic memory or something that they did to make you feel loved and appreciated. Then set the intention to remain open receiving more of the same as you journey together.

The Due Date

"I whispered, 'I love you'. I hope you heard before you left." ~ Zoe Clark-Coates

I woke my husband up just as the night gave way to the first morning light and we began our day with a sunrise picnic. We ate fruit and cocktail snacks, enjoyed a delicious aromatic cup of coffee, and a course, we also had a slice of birthday cake as we watched the sun ascend over the ocean. It's always so amazing how the calm of the ocean seeps into my soul and makes everything in my world feel okay. I felt that if I could drink in the powerful fluid essence of its vibrant waves beating against the shore then I could somehow gather the strength to face whatever was in front of me. Goodness knows how much I needed that strength just to survive what the year had presented me with. It was refreshing to feel so good, so close to one another and to be certain that this is exactly where we were meant to be at such a testing time.

I gave my husband two birthday gifts. The first was a message-in-a-bottle that held in it a scroll of messages from all his family and close friends. I welled up seeing how moved he was when he read all their heartfelt messages. Each of the love notes and birthday wishes reminded him of how loved he was and how many good, caring people there were in his life. My husband is a truly warm and giving person, so I was grateful to everyone who pitched in to help me create a little treasure that expressed their appreciation for him. The second gift was a certificate for two trees that I had planted in the Platbos Indigenous Forest in the Western Cape. One tree was planted to commemorate my husband's 40th birthday. The second tree was planted in remembrance of the precious baby soul that we didn't get to meet. It was a rough space to steer through because even in our moments of celebration, there was a thread of sadness too. We didn't want our angel baby's due date to go unmarked, so planting the tree seemed like a nice way to honour their memory. It was a way to satisfy the strong need we had to make sure that our baby's presence wasn't forgotten.

I'd hoped that the day would be different. I'd wanted to throw a big birthday party to celebrate him. I'd wanted my husband to spend the day surrounded by friends and family, and for him to know just how much we all loved him. The last thing I wanted was for our loss and the fact that our baby would have been due on his birthday to overshadow this significant milestone in his life. Yet, my husband had refused. He didn't want a party. He wanted a simple beach gateway, just the two of us. I felt guilty about it for a long time. I felt as though I was the source of constant pain. So, I fought his request as much as I could. I tried my best to convince him that we needed to have a big celebration. Still, he refused. In the end I accepted defeat and we booked a week long gateway at one of his favourite coastal cottages on the warm subtropical East Coast. Strangely, from the moment we arrived there, it became increasingly clear that it was actually precisely what we both needed. As my body relaxed and my breath synchronized with the calming rhythm of the waves, I quickly came to appreciate my husband's wisdom and foresight. This was our happy place. It was bound to offer us both respite.

After enjoying our little breakfast picnic beneath the stunning display that the morning sky offered, shifting from streaks of soft grey to vibrant hues of pink and blue, we went back to bed for a little while. We figured that we'd catch a little more sleep before going down to the beach for the day. We could not have asked for better weather when we headed out later that morning. It turned out to be a spectacularly sunny day. The late spring weather whispered to us that a sweltering summer was on its way, and the thought of it excited me. Down at the beach, I felt like a child again, frolicking in the waves and surrounded by a vast expanse of blue. The tide was in, so we took full advantage of the salt water pools, swimming and floating about. My body drifting to and fro with the rise and fall of the waves felt liberating. When we'd tired ourselves out, my husband and I found a nice quiet spot on the shore to settle down and soak up some sun. The sea breeze felt like a gentle warm current brushing through my hair. The beads of seawater, speckled all over my body, evaporated quickly. My heart was serene, by body was limber with every muscle relaxed. We sat in silence for a while, just watching the waves and sipping on the cathartic atmosphere.

"I love just sitting here and looking at the ocean," my husband said, *"It makes me think."*

"What are you thinking about?" I enquired.

"I've been reflecting on what my life has been like over the past 40 years," He responded.

His deep brown thought-soaked eyes turned their attention away from the scenic horizon to focus themselves on me.

"So much has happened," he continued, *"Fine, there are things that may not have worked out the way that I wanted them to, and there are also so many things that I still want to achieve, but for the most part I just feel so grateful."*

Emotions rose as he took my hand in his, in the reassuring manner that he always does.

"Most of all, I am grateful that I have been able to share my life with you."

"It's been a tough year for both of us with everything that transpired. I don't think you realize just how scared I was to lose you when the ectopic surgery happened," he said.

We spoke for a long time about the baby that we'd lost and how our ectopic pregnancy affected us. My husband told me how hard it was to see me in pain and how he worried that I blamed myself and wouldn't be able to forgive myself. He wasn't wrong. From the instant the doctor broke the news to us I'd immediately searched my mind for what I'd done to cause it. I told myself that I must have done something wrong. Self-blame was a quiet little voice always lurking somewhere at the back of my mind. I could almost forget about it until it pounced when I felt most vulnerable. It's that voice in me that whispers:

"It's my fault."

"It's my fault, because he could have had children by now if it wasn't for me. I am standing in the way of his happiness."

These thoughts always stung, they were painful mirrors of my inadequacies. At times when I'd vocalised the thoughts of self-blame that echoed in the recesses of my mind, or when I'd gotten angry at myself and told my husband that I wished he'd married someone else instead of me because he'd probably have a family that way, he'd say:

"Don't talk to or about my wife that way!"

Referring to me in the third person was a quick reminder that I am someone dear to him and that although I may find it hard to love myself in that particular moment, my self-critical thoughts are harmful to someone that he loves and values. Seeing this forced me to disassociate from my negative internal dialogue and evaluate how I was treating myself. My husband has been good at reaffirming the things I forget when I'm lost in self-loathing – that our situation is one of circumstance and that blaming myself for it won't change anything. He's always said that he and I *are a family* whether we have children or not, that we chose to be with one another, and that we are in this together, regardless of the outcome. The reassurance has helped pull me out of the clutches of self-blame. I am deeply appreciative of his compassionate nature, though it was also important for me to learn how to offer myself more kindness and to reframe my self-perception without the need for external reassurance too. So, during my healing journey I had to keep challenging myself to find my own ways to feel at peace with 'me', to not feel like I had 'bad' energy or my body was broken and I'd caused my baby to die. It wasn't easy, but I owed that to myself. I wanted to feel whole again, more able to love and accept myself. I spent time working on rebuilding my sense of self-worth and learning how to move beyond the self-blame to practice self-compassion instead.

Sitting on the beach with sand between our toes, our heels sinking deeper as the shifting sand grains gave way under the weight of our feet, we gathered two seagull feathers that were close by. We each held a feather in our hand and focused on releasing whatever we felt most shackled by. The feather represented the things we felt ready to let go of.

"What do you want to release?" We asked one another.

I focused on letting go of the hurt, the guilt, the self-blame and the emotional weight that kept me stuck. When we were ready, we released our feathers into the wind. We watched as they blew off into the mid-morning sky carrying with them the things that we no longer needed. It was a lovely symbolic exercise that felt like a positive step forward.

Still enjoying our comfortable spot along the shore, our conversation shifted to one of the main reasons my husband had wanted to come to the coast. It wasn't just about having the space to reflect on what had been. It was also about having a sense of looking forward. So, we took some time to explore some pertinent questions – *What did we want the next 40 years of our lives together to look like? What did we want more of going forward?* We allowed ourselves to dream as we discussed the vision we had for our life. I realized that I hadn't let myself think about the future much since our loss, so it felt really uplifting to speak about our hopes and plans, to paint a picture of our future home, family and the various goals that we wanted to see come to fruition. Exploring these questions was a necessary departure from grieving what we'd lost. It allowed us to get excited about what was still to come again.

As lunch time drew closer, we packed up to head back to our cottage. We had a reservation at an amazing seafood restaurant for our celebratory meal. When we stood up, I noticed a beautifully smoothed pearlescent piece of seashell at my feet. I picked it up, marveling at the stunning colours and tints that danced across the broken shell piece as it glistened in the sunlight. I turned the shell over in my hand and was so surprised by what I discovered. The back of the shell piece had on it a pattern that resembled a tiny foetus. I had gooseflesh. I starred at the pearlescent shell in the palm of my hand. It felt like a message from our spirit baby, a reassuring reminder that they were with us. It was like discovering a missing sherd that fit right into the hole in my heart, mending my soul a little more. I held the shell in my hand for most of that day, drawing comfort from it, unable to shake the feeling that this was a sign that our baby would come in divine time, when they were ready. There was magic about and I found myself more able to trust that everything would come together when it was meant to.

Later that afternoon, we sat on the veranda back at our cottage, sipping some sparkling apple juice and enjoying the view. I noticed several splashes out at sea. I got up to take a closer look and was amazed to see a massive school of wild dolphins in the water. It was an incredible sight. There could easily have been more than 50 of them. I'd never seen so many together in one place. The wild dolphins appeared joyful, jumping and playing while they swam. We watched them for a good 20 minutes. They gave us a wonderful show. My husband told me that they made him think of family, because they were essentially a big ocean family swimming together. Something about that felt like another message of hope for us. Once more, I felt comforted, grateful and connected to both our spirit baby and a greater spiritual force too.

Mending Softly Exercise

Ways To Honour Your Baby On Their Due Date

Light a candle. Take some time to reflect, grieve and process your loss. Write a letter to your baby. Talk about it with your partner, and give yourself the space to acknowledge and release whatever you need to.

Release a balloon. You can plan a small ceremony to release a balloon (or a few balloons) together with your partner or a close friend/family member. If you like, you can read a poem or say a few heartfelt words and then release the balloon.

Get a piece of jewellery. Get a special necklace, pendant, a charm or bracelet as a way to remember you baby. Some people choose an angel wing or a heart-shaped pendant, others choose a gemstone for their particular birth month. If you like, you could also get a piece of personalised jewellery made.

Plant a perennial plant or tree. Plant a tree or plant in your garden or have one planted at a nature park depending on what works best for you. Certain plants have specific meanings, and some flower at particular times of the year. For instance, amaryllis where my grandfather's favourite flower. Shortly before he passed away, he got a few amaryllis bulbs for my grandmother to plant in her flowerbed. She in turn gave me a couple of those bulbs to plant in my garden. These bulbs always bloom in September. September happens to be my grandfather's birthday month, and the same month when he passed away. So whenever my amaryllis bloom, I think of and feel close to him.

Post Traumatic Growth

"The Wound is the Place Where the Light Enters You"

~ Rumi

Waves break. They crash and beat against black rocks. They whip against the undulating shores and toss themselves about in their wild and stormy ways. But after their violent unbecoming, their big bewildering exhale is followed by the gentle rush of the sea pulling itself back together. It's like a healing intake of breath, inhaling the calm of life back into itself and returning to wholeness. Along my road to recovery after my ectopic pregnancy, I came to understand this is a metaphor for life. It is a cyclical dance of breaking and mending. We shatter and heal. We crash, burn and then revive ourselves. No matter how broken we feel, when the wheel slowly turns again, we find ourselves coming full circle on our journey back to inner harmony, back to our spiritual centre. It's refreshing when that time comes, when you wake up one day and see that *'Hey, I'm still here'....'I never really left'...'I've just been waiting for my wounds to heal well enough in order for me to gather the courage to live fully again'.*

When you've reached this place, your inner 'pottery mender', an embodiment of the archetypical nurturer, is offered a moment to pause, step back and reflect. Perhaps for the first time throughout your healing process she has the chance to see how far you have come. She may start to notice things that escaped her attention before, while you were still in survival mode and she was doing the demanding work of piecing the fragments of 'self' back together. From this position of pause, it becomes easier to notice the lessons and perhaps to find meaning in things too. You see a little more clearly how you have grown through it all, how you have cultivated strength in spirit in ways that once seemed inconceivable. Your back straightens up, your eyes regain their sparkle and the weight of the world is no longer crushing your spine the way it did when you were in the thick of your period of tumult. You're suddenly acutely aware of how you've rebuilt yourself as a person, day by day, week by week, tirelessly remolding the shape of your body and soul.

I found myself in this pensive state of pause at the end of our long and challenging year. My husband and I were fortunate to get a chance to take another trip down to the coast. It was mid-summer and as usual, the natural beauty of our surrounds became a place of sanctuary, giving us space to check in with and locate ourselves after a long hard road. As we combed the beach, swam in the ocean, birdwatched and hiked along an incredible mountain river trail, I noticed that I was also discovering the parts of myself that had grown and surfaced both in spite of and as a consequence of our pregnancy loss. It was a strange feeling. I was deeply grounded and grateful for the harmonious flow that I was uncovering within myself. Early one morning, while my husband was still asleep, I sat on the veranda and listened to the familiar whispers of the sea breeze. I was conscious of how I was learning to be at peace in my own body again. I watched the as rising sun melted away the layers of grey clouds and mist that I'd woken up to. As I jotted down my morning musings in my journal, there was a strong sense of nostalgia that I couldn't shake. I searched my mind for clues as to what felt so familiar about this particular sunrise. Then it struck me. A few years earlier, I sat outside on this very veranda, watching a similar scene unfold. It was an early morning after we'd had a gloomy thunderstorm the night before, just like this. I suddenly remembered the words that came to me as I poured my internal stirrings onto my journal pages that day, musings that I would later share on my blog under the title, 'The wholeness of the wild sea'. Here is what I wrote:

After last night's rain, the sky is a patchy tapestry of pale blue and fluffy grey clouds. The once stormy black ocean now glistens like sheets of molten gold. The world has transformed itself into a new day.

What did it have to lose, surrender and release for it to be so?

What did it have to gain, accept and carry forward for it to be as it is now?

We will never really know the wild magic of night that unfolds while we sleep. Our minds know only what we see. I guess that is the gift of living from the heart, because the wise heart knows the unseen. It taps into mystery. It seeks out beauty and sacredness. It intuitively traces pieces of wildness along unseen paths to secret worlds of deep and feral magic.

That place within us, the heart, the wild essence, knows the transformative path that the black night ocean has had to take to become the illuminated body of light that I see on the horizon. And it knows too, the path that our own souls need to take from dark and stormy places of brokenness to the healing light of love.

These words that I'd penned many moons ago appeared profoundly relevant in my present context. I spent some time contemplating them in relation to my recovery after loss. I knew what I'd lost and how I had to surrender. Now, I felt steady and whole enough to look closer at what I had gained. There is a poignant verse in Antonio Machado's poem, 'Last Night As I Was Sleeping', that reads as follows:

> *"Last night as I was sleeping,*
> *I dreamt—marvelous error!—*
> *that I had a beehive*
> *here inside my heart.*
> *And the golden bees*
> *were making white combs*
> *and sweet honey*
> *from my old failures."*

It was such a beautiful visual that really resonated in that moment. What white combs and sweet honey had the golden bees of life made out of the grief and turmoil of our tumultuous year? How had I grown through my trauma?

Sitting calmly on the other side of my storm, I could see that there were many lessons that I'd learnt about life and about myself too. The gift of sweet and sticky honey had drizzled over and seeped into my soul in various ways. Although my pregnancy didn't work out, the fact that I fell pregnant when I did taught me to trust my intuition and to believe in possibilities. It affirmed to me that although the time wasn't right, I was still moving in the right direction. Despite my fears of inadequacy, those early weeks of pregnancy taught me to trust that I am a good mother who will make the best decisions for my baby's wellbeing. I ate well to nourish my baby, committed to a regular practice of gentle exercise and sent my baby as much positive energy as possible so that they would know that they were loved and welcome. I recognized that my period of early pregnancy was a gift, especially considering many women in this situation don't even have a chance to acknowledge, celebrate or enjoy the idea of being pregnant. I did, and that was something to be grateful for.

In the midst of my stormy winter, I looked my greatest fear in the eye and faced it. I surrendered, lost control and I didn't die, even when it felt like I might. I came face to face with many of the limiting beliefs that I held about myself and was forced to confront and work on relinquishing them in a manner that I didn't have the courage to before. I learned how to nurture myself and how to lean into self-compassion when I was struggling to find the strength to navigate the hardest days. I learned to love myself at my worst. The need to prioritize myself and my healing taught me to open up and allow myself to be loved and supported, and to get better at asking for help and allowing myself to receive. Quite importantly, it also showed me how to set better boundaries and to be more conscious of the energy and people that I allow into my space. This was a much needed shift that created balance in my relationships and friendships. It showed me how strong the foundation of our marriage is and deepened our connection to one another. I will never tire of expressing just how grateful I am for my loving and supportive husband who has made even the worst days more bearable. One thing that I keep going back to, perhaps because it reflects qualities I didn't think I had in me, is that surviving my trauma revealed to me my vast well of inner strength and resilience. I'd never thought of myself as a strong person. This experience challenged and forced me to dig deep. It called me to show up for myself and transformed the way I perceive myself for the better. For a period of time, I lost trust in my body, and I lost trust in Spirit too. I worked hard to restore that connection and found my way back to spiritual harmony. When I thought about the fact that things could have been worse – I could have lost my own life, but I didn't – it was hard not to feel that as shitty as the situation was, I was still held and protected by a greater force. Perhaps my life had value, even when at times I couldn't see it. Although I didn't fully understand why things happened as they did, I did come to trust in the highest good. I'd struggled to believe that this sort of thing 'happened for a reason', but I did realize that I could choose to find meaning in my tragedy. I could also choose to give meaning to the life of my angel baby. I felt that I owed them that for the precious moments of joy they brought me during that short period of time. In his book, 'Man's Searching for Meaning', Austrian psychiatrist and Holocaust survivor, Viktor Frankl said that *"In some ways suffering ceases to be suffering at the moment it finds a meaning."* I personally found truth in this. Beyond finding meaning in the midst of suffering and trauma, the resilience-building practices that I turned to helped my growth too. It led me to a place where I could look back and see the nuggets of good that came with the bad. When I was at my lowest point, my goal was merely to be okay enough to keep breathing through the pain. I'd hardly expected that I would one day feel more empowered or have a new lease on life. I didn't think it would be possible to go from survival mode to feeling like the spirit in me was thriving again. I found that trauma has a way of sifting through the bullshit and putting things into perspective. Your pseudo-values fall to the wayside, you learn what matters most to you and that allows you to simplify life in a way. As you redirect your attention away from whatever doesn't serve you and towards your highest good, you make peace with what you cannot change. This doesn't invalidate your grief. Acknowledging, feeling and processing these things are part of your healing. However, when you accept that you can't change what has happened, you learn to focus more on what heals, inspires and helps you grow. Your energy expands. Light enters your heart. You see what nourishes you and you focus on what gives purpose and meaning. In the words of Viktor Frankl:

"We must never forget that we may also find meaning in life even when confronted with a hopeless situation, when facing a fate that cannot change. For what then matters is to bear witness to the uniquely human potential at its best, which is to transform a personal tragedy into a triumph, to

turn one's predicament into a human achievement. When we are no longer able to change a situation – just think of an incurable disease such as inoperable cancer – we are challenged to change ourselves."

This experience changed me profoundly. Looking back I could now see what I had rebuilt myself into – the sherds carefully placed together, their edges smoothed and tightly glued to remake myself anew. Perhaps the treasure in reclaiming my scattered pieces was more about the journey that I walked when I was slowly mending. My unbecoming brought with it unexpected growth and evolution. My healing journey taught me that it was important to allow the skin of my soul to take new form, morph and become what it is now, not what it was once was. It taught me that this is how we heal, this is how we grow, and for that I am grateful.

Affirmation

"I trust in the journey. I am always learning and growing. I trust that each step I take forward brings me closer and closer to my highest good."

Writing Prompt

Finding the Light Beyond the Trauma

Reflect on the following questions. Explore the insights that come up for you and write about them in your journal:

When you look back at what you have been through, what has it taught you?

What did you learn about yourself? What qualities did surviving your loss allow you to unearth within yourself?

Has this experience helped you to grow in any way? If so, how?

Making Room for Hope

"Water your heart's seeds with hope. Nurture what you love. How else will the important things flourish?"

~ *The Fertile Moon*

When I walked into the warm breezy room I was immediately overcome with a mix of emotions. Late summer's afternoon sun poured in generously through the window. The white cotton curtains danced on the breeze in somewhat etheric fashion. This room has always had a sense of softness to it. Its coolness offered respite from the heat. It felt uplifting, filled with light and hope. Yet, it also has a touch of emptiness too, probably because its intended purpose has yet to be fulfilled. I looked across at the wall near the blowing curtains where I've hung a decorative mobile. It's a colourful string of four animals made from vibrant patterned African fabric. My husband and I bought it at a Maasai market in Zanzibar while on holiday a couple of years ago. I guess it was what some may call a 'faith purchase', something special for our future baby's room to help keep the doors of hope open.

I sat down on the couch and reveled in the comforting sensation of toasty golden sunrays. And for a moment my mind drifted to the place it often tends to wonder off to whenever I settle down in that spot. I visualised it all so clearly. I could see my future baby in my arms, their tiny head resting on my chest and moving gently to the rhythm of the rise and fall of my breath. I'd often catch myself wondering what it will feel like when our baby is finally here. Here in the flesh, here in this room. What will it feel like to know that they are mine, to know that I am their mother? What will it be like to nurse and nurture my baby? For several moments I'm lost to the idea of these magical possibilities.

People sometimes talk about how rooms hold memories and how walls are silent witnesses to the happenings of our daily lives. Perhaps one day I'll look back at this room in reflection of its past and the heartwarming ways in which it served me, but for now it offers a glimpse at the future that we aspire to. It is a window peering into the things that we are dreaming into being and keeps me mindful of the meaningful experiences that I want to invite into my life. At present, this room is our home office. It houses a cozy couch and beautiful wooden writing desk that we had custom made by a talented carpenter just before he retired from making furniture. The draws and cupboards in the room are filled with files, important paperwork and office supplies. Yet in its quiet corners and hidden spaces are little love notes and gentle nudges of hope. Like the wall-hanging mobile that I mentioned, and the special shelf in the cupboard that I've cleared to make space for the things we've collected for our one-day-baby. Books I'd love to read to them, a couple of soft toys, a baby blanket, a few cute onesies and the pre-conception journal that my husband and I write notes and letters to our future child in.

If this room had a memory I'd want it to tell the story of our hope in waiting. Leaving traces of the function that we dream this room will eventually serve – for it to finally become our baby's room – feels comforting. It gives me peace knowing that I am putting a message out there, an invitation of sorts, one that says: *"We love you. We welcome you. We have created the space for you in our lives in the meantime."* I always want my child to know just how much they were wanted long before they arrived, and I endeavor to keep kindling the feelings of hope and to create space for them in my life, physically, mentally and emotionally. It takes an incredible amount of faith to trust in the future, but I believe in happy endings, as imperfect as they may sometimes be. To draw from the words of Christina Oberon, author of Hope Strong: Navigating the Emotions of Your Infertility Journey: *"Hope is a constant pillar even in your darkest hour."*

Writing Prompt

What makes you feel hopeful?

How do you create space for hope along your fertility journey?

What keeps you connected to the heartwarming possibility of eventually bringing your baby into your life?

Acknowledgements

I offer my heartfelt gratitude to you, the reader for allowing me space in your life and for letting my words into your heart. May you find hope, healing and grace on your journey.

Thank you to my husband and soulmate, Cyrus Rogers, for your unconditional love, gentleness and for always being a solid rock for me to lean on when I am at my weakest.

I thank our family and friends who have been a positive and supportive presence in the midst of our turmoil.

Thank you to Amy, Asanda, Gugulethu, Jocelyn, Nomalanga, Pralene, Rosa and Thobile, my beautiful soul sisters and support system who always show up for me. Each of you hold a very special place in my heart. I appreciate your sisterhood.

A special thank you to the Bimrays, the Chamas and the Dikobos for being there for us during a really difficult time.

To Twatasha and Chama, thank you for the light and joy that your presence always brings into our lives.

To our 'big brother', Kaunda, thank you for being a confidant, and a patient, wise and gentle soul for the both of us to lean on.

Thank you to my wellness coach, Sandra, and Naturopath, Leanne, for helping me to restore and enhance my fertility and overall wellness.

Thank you to Marj, Tiffany, Carol, Sheralee and the ladies at Our Movement Studio for creating a beautiful place of healing, one that offered sanctuary when I needed it most.

Bibliography

Books

Broken Places & Outer Spaces, Simon & Schuter, Nnedi Okorafor, 2019

Daring to Rest: Reclaim Your Power with Yoga Nidra Rest Meditation, Karen Brody, Sounds True, 2017

Hope Strong: Navigating the Emotions of Your Infertility Journey, KOKO Press, Christina Oberon, 2019

Infertility and PTSD – The Uncharted Storm, Joanna Flemons, Createspace Independent Publishing, 2018

Man's Searching for Meaning, Viktor E. Frankl, Beacon Press, 2006

Tending the Earth, Mending the Spirit: The Healing Gifts of Gardening, Connie Goldman & Richard Mahler, Nodin Press, 2000

The Baby Loss Guide, Zoe Clark-Coates, Orion, 2019

The Universe Has Your Back, Gabrielle Bernstein, Hay House, 2016

Wild Comfort: The Solace of Nature, Kathleen Dean Moore, Trumpeter Books, 2010

Wild Feminine: Finding Power, Spirit & Joy in the Female Body, Tami Lynn Kent, Beyond Words, 2011

Yes, You Can Get Pregnant, Demos Medical Publishing, by Aimee E. Raupp, 2014

Articles, Blogs, Websites

On Mending Pottery

Mending Those Humble Sherds, Lives and Legacies Blog: Link: https://livesandlegaciesblog.org/2015/02/25/mending-broken-pots/

The Art of Repairing Broken Ceramics Creates a New Kind of Beauty, Evan Nichole Brown, Atlas Obscura Article, Link: https://www.atlasobscura.com/articles/repairing-broken-ceramics

Simply Riveting: Broken and Mended Ceramics, Angelika R. Kuettner, Chipstone Article, Link: http://www.chipstone.org/article.php/742/Ceramics-in-America-2016/Simply-Riveting:-Broken-and-Mended-Ceramics

Broken Pots: More than the Sum of their Parts, Lotte Govaerts, Rogers Archeology Lab, Link: https://nmnh.typepad.com/rogers_archaeology_lab/2015/04/broken-pots-more-than-the-sum-of-their-parts.html

On Gardening Therapy

Monty Don on Gardening for Mental Health Wellness:
https://www.telegraph.co.uk/news/2019/02/24/gardening-can-do-medicine-tries-mimic-mental-health-monty-don/

Green shoots: 'gardening provides welcome relief from my infertility':
https://www.theguardian.com/lifeandstyle/2017/nov/11/gardens-tending-veg-and-flowers-brings-comfort-after-ivf

Grief, PTSD and Healing

How Does Yoga Help with PTSD, Wolf Terry, Yoga Journal, July 2020. Link: https://www.yogajournal.com/yoga-101/how-does-yoga-help-with-ptsd

How We Contribute to Disenfranchising the Grief of Pregnancy Loss, Angie Plews, Harmonious Minds Women's Mental Health, Link: https://www.harmoniousminds.com.au/how-we-contribute-to-disenfranchising-the-grief-of-pregnancy-loss/

Spiritual Guru Gabby Bernstein On Mothering Herself And The Power Of Healing Her Gut, Baby Hatch, Link: https://babebyhatch.com/spiritual-guru-gabby-bernstein-on-mothering-herself/

Mending Softly

Front Cover Design: Jodi Sky Rogers

Author Photograph by: Melissa Hogarth

About Author

Jodi Sky Rogers is a Feminine Healing/Fertility Support Coach and Author. Her personal experience with PCOS, Fertility challenges and Pregnancy Loss over the past seven years inspires her to support women going through similar experiences. She is passionate about creating soulful fertility, mindfulness and TTC self-care resources and tools to support women on their fertility journey. She is a fertility blogger for the Conceive IVF Gynaecology & Fertility Hospital's 'Fried Eggs & Slow Swimmers' blog. She is the author of everal books, including: Flowering Within, Wild Essence, Daily Cup of Fertility Calm and the Fertility Calm Creative Journal.

Website: http://jodiskyrogers.com

Instagram: @thefertilemoon

Mending Softly

Printed in Great Britain
by Amazon